There's Something I've Been Dying to Tell You

Lynda Bellingham

CORONET

First published in Great Britain in 2014 by Coronet
An imprint of Hodder & Stoughton
An Hachette UK company

4

Copyright © Lynda Bellingham 2014

The right of Lynda Bellingham to be identified as the Author of the Work has been
asserted by her in accordance with the Copyright, Designs and Patents Act 1988.

A CIP catalogue record for this title is available from the British Library

ISBN 9781473608566
Trade Paperback ISBN 9781473608573
Ebook ISBN 9781473608559

Typeset by Hewer Text UK Ltd, Edinburgh
Printed and bound by Clays Ltd, St Ives plc

Hodder & Stoughton policy is to use papers that are natural, renewable
and recyclable products and made from wood grown in sustainable
forests. The logging and manufacturing processes are expected to
conform to the environmental regulations of the country of origin.

Hodder & Stoughton Ltd
338 Euston Road
London NW1 3BH

www.hodder.co.uk

The photographs on page 4 of the first picture section are
reproduced with kind thanks to Julie Phelan/Shop Direct.
Picture on page 8 of the second picture section by
Brian Aris courtesy of *Yours* magazine

"Happy Talk"
Copyright © 1949 by Richard Rodgers and Oscar Hammerstein II
Copyright Renewed
Williamson Music, an Imagem Company, owner of
publication and allied rights throughout the World
International Copyright Secured. All Rights Reserved. Used by Permsission

There's Something
I've Been Dying to Tell You

Words will never express my love for my husband, Michael, nor my sons Michael and Robbie, nor indeed my stepson Bradley who has arrived at a strange time in his life and mine. I love you so much and just want you to be happy. You will be and I will be cheering you on. Take no notice of the tears, they are just a girl thing, and I am saluting the boy thing.

Forever and always.

Respect and don't take shit from anyone.

x

ACKNOWLEDGEMENTS

....

There are so many people involved in the story within this book and I am so moved by how much work and care they have for patients and people in general. I guess I should start at the top of the tree with Professor Justin Stebbing and his team headed up by Lesley Bedford. Then all the wonderful nurses at the London Clinic and the two stars at Leaders in Oncology Care: Clare Cobbett and Ani Ransley.

My thanks go to dear Dr di Cesare and all the Macmillan Cancer care team. Thank you to my dear sister Jean for all her love and care and to Kathryn Peel at Ophir Travel who has managed to bring sunshine into my life through places like Marbella and Corfu. Finally to the wonderful Charlotte Hardman and her team at Hodder and Stoughton for believing in me and publishing this book. I do hope it brings some enlightenment to those who are still asking the question 'Why?'!

Keep your friends close and love them dearly – they are the best acknowledgements one can ever have. Life affirming.

*'The most stupid cancer cell
is cleverer than the brightest oncologist.'*

PROLOGUE

....

'Cancer, what do you mean cancer?' I asked in amazement.

The very pleasant gentleman in front of my husband and me visibly crumpled in his seat. He stared at his computer for a few seconds and then seemed to pull himself up and looked me straight in the eye.

'I am so terribly sorry I thought you had already been informed of your position. You have cancer of the colon, and lesions on your lungs and your liver.'

I cannot write what this moment was like effectively. I have tried so many different ways to put it into words and it is just not possible. Anyone in this position, as I was at that moment, might possibly agree with me when I say I felt nothing except disbelief. Me? Cancer? Never.

It had never occurred to me I would die of cancer. Heart failure, maybe, liver damage quite possibly, but not cancer. How stupid is that? The statistics suggest that one in three people die of cancer . . .

My mind was starting to wander. I was suddenly aware of Michael, my dear darling husband, sobbing in the chair next to me. I put my hand on his arm and said, 'Don't cry, darling, it is going to be alright.' I turned back to the doctor and switched into actress mode. It was ridiculous!

'Well, there's a turn up for the books. Cancer? That bloody private doctor didn't tell us a thing. I even asked him, didn't I, Michael? "Is it cancer?" I said. "Oh no I am sure it is nothing like that," he said. Why didn't he tell us there and then?'

Mr Richard Cohen, the surgeon in front of us, looked uncomfortable and replied, 'Well, I am sure he had his reasons. The point is, Lynda, we need to get on and do something about your state of health pretty quickly.'

'Can't you operate?' said Michael, who had composed himself and was back to being supportive. Thank God, because everything that was discussed in the next twenty minutes went in one ear and out the other as far as I was concerned.

'Well yes and no,' came the reply. 'I am a surgeon and it is my job to remove tumours. I am a bit like a glorified plumber,' said Mr Cohen. 'But in your case, Lynda, it is imperative that you see an oncologist first, and see one as soon as possible. I have made an appointment for you to go and see Professor Justin Stebbing when we are finished here. He is at the London Oncology Clinic at number 95, just down the road. You are very fortunate he is around because I consider him to be one of the best in his field.'

Mr Cohen then introduced us to his team, and a lovely lady went through some of the basic questions. Weirdly, perhaps, the one thing we didn't ask at the time was 'Is it terminal?' I think we just assumed it was; like everyone does, don't they? Cancer = death.

We found ourselves out on the street, Harley Street to be precise. This world-famous street lined with gorgeous rows of elegant houses with glossy front doors and sparkling brass knockers, behind which some of the greatest doctors in the world are gathered, practising every kind of medicine. As we walked from number 116 to number 95 we held each other and tried so hard to stop the tears from flowing. All around us people were hurrying to and fro and horns blared. Life goes on. We bowed our heads and turned into each other as though protecting ourselves from a storm.

We arrived at the clinic and presented ourselves at the desk. There were beautiful flowers on display and a big bowl of sweets on the desk. I took one automatically and the receptionist gave me a big smile, 'Can't resist them? Neither can I.' She indicated two seats and explained the professor would be with us shortly.

We sat down and I looked around the quiet room. Everywhere I looked there was evidence of this dreadful disease. Heads shaved or covered in colourful scarves. Faces drawn and hollow. Husbands and wives holding hands tightly and smiling bravely at each other. Others sitting alone, erect and defiant. I felt nothing. Just empty and still disbelieving. What was I doing here? I cast a sideways glance at Michael, who was staring at his phone, pushing buttons.

I suddenly wanted to curl up and go to sleep. Always my way of dealing with things, and I would probably have nodded off right there had the receptionist not called us to go up to the second floor. We climbed a beautiful oak staircase sheathed in thick expensive carpet and found ourselves in front of a huge door. It was like being summoned to the headmaster's study – but then the door was opened by someone who looked more like the head boy, he seemed so young!

'Hi! I am Justin, please come in and take a seat. May I call you Lynda?' he asked, as he sat down opposite us behind a huge desk with a computer screen inlaid in the top. I was very impressed.

'Can I just say before we go through all the details that this must be a terrible shock for you both and nothing will make sense, but it is important you understand that having cancer does not mean you are going to die, Lynda.'

Michael sat back in his chair and put his head in his hands and let out a gasp. I just turned into a diva and declared, 'Well, you are bound to say that, but can I just tell you I don't want to spend years wandering round with no hair feeling like shit and upsetting my family just to prolong the agony for a couple of years.'

Michael was crying again now and I wanted to scream at them to stop it. I could not let the professor give me all the usual placatory bullshit and I did not want Michael crying because of me, that was accepting the inevitable and at that point in time I was not prepared to accept anything. I just did not want to think about it. I just could not keep a coherent thought in my head.

Professor Stebbing was not amused by my outburst. 'Stop it immediately, Lynda. That is not what I want to be hearing and I am sure Michael doesn't either. I am the

4

expert and I am telling you now that the advance in the treatment of certain cancers has moved so fast that unless you are in the centre of it, as I am, you cannot possibly appreciate how far we have come. Now let me tell you what we are going to do with you.'

He then explained he was going to blast me with the strongest chemotherapy they had. A mixture of Avastin and Oxaliplatin and the fabulous fluorouracil, also gloriously known as 'FU2'.

How wonderful is that? From that moment on I christened my cancer FU2.

Justin explained that it seemed likely I had had the tumour for at least eighteen months. So much for the stool test I religiously take every year. As Richard Cohen had anticipated, instead of operating, Justin thought I needed to start the chemotherapy as soon as possible as there were secondaries on the lungs and the liver.

'Maybe a few months down the line we can reconsider your options, but at this time I want to get on and attack the problem.'

Justin was speaking into a microphone, recording everything as if I was not in the room. Things seemed to be moving so fast and I had a horrible sense of losing control of my life. He explained that I would go in to the clinic on the following day and I would have a colonoscopy. They would also insert a port in my chest to take the drip for chemo and I would be having a scan. Then on the Friday I would start my first chemotherapy session.

I smiled and nodded inanely at everything I was told, and poor Michael tried very hard to make sure he had all the facts. God knows what I would have been like if he hadn't been there to pay attention.

I had this huge lump in my throat and a desire to burst into tears, but somehow did not want to be embarrassing. I wanted this man in front of me to know that I was strong and could take anything he threw at me. I was not going to succumb to actressy wobbles and tantrums. I was a proper person who could cope with anything. I thought, being there in that room was like getting the acting job of the century. How deluded can a girl be?

We found ourselves back out on the street once more. The sun was shining, and as I looked towards Cavendish Square I could see that bastion of middle-class comfort and joy: John Lewis. Whenever I walked into that store as a young woman I felt I was somehow starting life on a rung of a ladder that only went up, and things would get better and better. I did not expect to arrive at the Harrods level of retail, nor did I want that, but John Lewis has always had aspirations. I know I must sound very middle class but then I am! My mother came from a lowly background but always aspired to do better, to have a lovely home, and where back in the day she would go to Marks and Spencer for her clothing, she would take trips up West to see what John Lewis was suggesting in the china and soft furnishings. It must have been incredible in those early years of the fifties when fridges and gadgets started to arrive. What extravagance.

How many times in the last forty years had I walked down this yellow brick road to happiness and shopping! I used to live around the corner when I was at drama school, and loved the elegance of my surroundings, even if I couldn't really afford any of it. I would wander down this road, eyes straight ahead to my goal: Oxford Street!

There was a wonderful moment when I was at drama school in 1968. I met Nickolas Grace on the first day at the Central School of Speech and Drama in 1966, and have stayed friends ever since. He got us invitations to a very special charity ball. He knew lots of famous actors because he was the president of the Redgrave Society at his school and he was always arranging things so that he could meet his idols! Anyway, the very famous Kenneth More was the guest of honour. For those of you under the age of sixty who may be reading this, Kenneth More became famous for playing a very brave pilot called Douglas Bader in the Second World War who lost his legs while fighting the Germans. The film was called *Reach for the Sky*.

It was a black tie event which does not pose a great problem for boys but for me it was a huge dilemma. Who at the age of twenty, and living on a grant at drama school, has an evening dress – unless of course you were born with a silver spoon in your gob! Well God moves in mysterious ways and one morning I was strolling down my favourite yellow brick road towards John Lewis, and for the first time ever I was looking right and left, scanning the shop windows for sparkly dresses. Suddenly the sunlight caught a sequin in a shop window and there waiting for me, waving at me, was the most incredible long silver sequined dress I have ever seen. It was a Shirley Bassey dress. I stood outside the shop and just devoured it from head to toe. A very jolly sales assistant was obviously watching me and she came to the door and said, 'Why don't you come in and try it on? No harm in that.'

I could not even find words to express my desire to pour myself into this confection of silver. I followed her into the shop to the changing room at the back. I took off my clothes and sat still as a statue waiting for the arrival of my fantasy. She slipped it over my head and it slithered down my body like a caress. It fitted perfectly, but I knew it would.

'Oh my dear, you look beautiful,' said the temptress. 'Is it a special occasion?'

Well that was it, a combination of nerves and excitement sent me into overdrive and I was telling her all about the 'do' and Kenneth More ('Oh I love him,' said the lady, adjusting the fishtail on my dress) and suddenly it was a done deal. Except I did not know the price of the dress and there was no way – even if I paid in instalments for the rest of my life – that I was going to be able to buy it. I started to pull it back over my head with the sales assistant still attached!

'I am so sorry,' I stammered, 'but I am wasting your time. There is no way I could pay for something like this.'

'You don't know that,' encouraged the Fairy Queen. 'Let's see . . . well for a start it is on "special offer" because there is a tiny nick in the fishtail here, look. But it is so small we can invisibly mend that easily. It is £50. Madam, that is cheap!'

'Not cheap enough I am afraid,' I said but a little voice was pushing its way to the surface: *You have to speculate to accumulate, don't you?*

I was lucky (or unlucky depending on which way you looked at it) to have a brilliant bank manager who I could talk to like a father. In fact he was my dad's bank manager also, and he had always been incredibly supportive, knowing how tough it was for farmers, like my family, starting up after the war. Maybe, just maybe, he would understand my predicament and give me a loan?

'Would it be possible to use your phone and ring my bank?' I ventured. Don't forget there were no mobile phones back then! 'Yes, be my guest,' said the she-devil, handing me the phone.

I tried to sneak into the corner of the changing room and whispered into the mouthpiece.

'Hi, is that you, Mr Wyatt? . . . Yes, I am fine, no I am whispering because I am in a dress shop and I want to ask . . . Dress shop. Yes it does sound ominous, doesn't it?! The thing is you always tell me to speculate to accumulate and I have the chance to make lots of contacts and possibly further my career.'

I explained about the evening and as soon as I mentioned Kenneth More he was impressed.

'How much is the dress?' he said, getting down to the nitty-gritty.

'Fifty pounds,' I said, as quickly as I could.

There was a very long silence and then I heard him smile . . . yes you can hear a smile, I promise you!

'Very well, Miss Bellingham, you may have the money but I want you to put a little money back each month for the repayment.'

I stifled a scream of joy and did a little dance in the changing cubicle.

'Thank you thank you thank you. I will send you a photo of the evening.'

I put the phone down and carried it back to the counter. 'Thank you, I will take the dress and please can we fix the small nick in the hem by next Saturday?'

'Certainly, of course, Madam, and may I say nothing gives me greater pleasure than being able to sell you this. You look stunning.'

I walked back up Marylebone High Street in a daze.

I had silver shoes – my practice dance shoes for movement class – which I could wear with the dress. They were not quite high enough but I could stand on tippy-toe all night if need be. Nothing was going to spoil this evening.

Nik and I were probably the youngest couple there that night and everyone commented on my dress. Mind you I was a little like a Christmas tree! I should have had an inkling of trouble ahead after the third person had stood on my flicked out fishtail but I just made myself stand taller. This was not quite the thing to do as Kenneth More was making his way towards me and he was not what you might call tall.

'How do you do? My name is Kenneth and I would like to ask for the next dance if I may,' said Mr More. He was very charming and had a definite twinkle in his eye.

'Thank you that would be lovely,' I demurred in my most ladylike manner.

He took my hand and sort of twirled me onto the dance floor to the opening bars of a waltz and another sound, a rather ragged note as if something was tearing . . . Oh my God, my dress! He was standing on my dress! It ripped from the rather flirty slit at the back straight up to my bra.

'I am so sorry, my dear, here take my jacket and cover yourself.' He handed me his dinner jacket.

If he had offered it for any other reason than to cover a rip, it would have been such a romantic gesture, but instead I ran from the ballroom to the cloakroom. I was in floods of tears and the poor cloakroom attendant had a job to calm me down. She was so sweet and produced a needle and thread and literally sewed me back into my frock. Now that is what I call service. I spent the rest of the night seated at the table, pretending to all and sundry that it was no big deal. Only a little repair and after all it was only a dress. Ha, only! It was a rent to my heart, and what would Mr Wyatt make of my disaster?

But would you believe it God took care of me, and the following week I was asked to do a voice-over for the TV for a carpet shop or something. My first ever voice-over and the fee would be £50! Cross my heart and hope to die. (Well, actually that is rather inappropriate now, isn't it?) I was able to send My Wyatt the money and my silver dress went into the dressing-up box at college.

Now though, standing there on Harley Street, suddenly I saw it all with new eyes. What is really important in life? Behind these beautiful facades, sickness lay. Every basement window with subtle blinds and opaque glass hid the real business of the day – people fighting for their lives. And although it is a cliché that money can't buy everything, a silver dress is nothing compared to your health.

Well, so be it. I made up my mind that if 95 Harley Street was to become my home for the next few months, it would be a place of pain and comfort, but most important of all . . . it would be a place of hope.

1
AND SO IT BEGAN

....

July 2013

I was admitted to the London Clinic LOC on 3 July for a colonoscopy. I certainly wasn't looking forward to it. During a colonoscopy, they basically put a small camera up your bum. You are not under general anaesthetic for the procedure, but they give you Valium and you can watch the proceedings on the screen to the side if you so desire. Personally I would rather keep my eyes closed and thoughts elsewhere on much more pleasant things, but a friend of mine, who is a very cheeky chappie, told me it was the best sex he had ever had!

I really don't remember much about it to be honest but Richard Cohen was able to see the damage. There were three tumours apparently. When it was over, Michael came to take me home and we went to the cinema. The next day I was back at the clinic for a heart cardiogram and then admitted to await my operation to put in a port. Any port in a storm! A port is an amazing invention and I would recommend it to anyone who is going to have to have chemo. It is a small disc implanted in the chest through which all the intravenous injections can be given. It sounds a bit toe-curling but, believe me, when one is having literally hundreds of injections it makes life so much easier and there is no pain at all. I sat on my bed in the London Clinic all afternoon watching TV until Mr Imberts arrived to tell me all about the procedure. I was back in bed within the hour ordering my supper.

Of course, I know, you may read this and think, 'Jammy woman on the private healthcare, what does she know?' Well, as a matter of fact, I do know both sides. When I was growing up I always spent my school holidays working at Stoke Mandeville Hospital. It was very new then and specialised, as it does still, in spinal cases. The nurses worked so hard and I loved the camaraderie of the nursing staff and their dedication to their jobs.

When I left drama school and became a self-employed person I quickly realised that I could never afford to be ill, I couldn't afford to take the time off work, and if I needed medical attention swiftly the poor old NHS was never going to deliver. Of course it does in real emergencies, one can have no better care, indeed it uses the same surgeons as one pays for in the private sector. But say I got a bug, or broke a bone while filming, then I needed to get it sorted quickly, and by having private healthcare I was able to deal with most eventualities. My friends thought I was mad paying out each month and, believe me, there were times when I had no money in the bank and I was living off boiled eggs and soldiers, but I never gave up the payments.

Years later I had a huge overdraft but great medical cover, and it has been a godsend this last year. Everything that has happened to me has been made a little easier to bear because of the amazing care, the speed with which I've been tended to and the comfort in which I've received my treatment. When you are in hospital you realise just how important the whole set-up is, from the surgeons to the nurses, to the healthcare workers, to the cleaners. I have met some amazing people from all these groups in the last year, and believe me they all deserve such praise.

So I was now sporting a small bump on my chest which would be accommodating an intravenous drip to carry the magic chemo up a tube under my skin. All you could see from the outside was what looked like a vein in the side of my neck and a small scar just above my right breast. I have never really been into plunging necklines so there was no danger of anyone noticing my impediment. I was prepped and ready for my first chemotherapy session the next day, on 5 July. As I am writing these words I glance at my watch and I realise it is exactly a year since I started this deadly affair with the disease that wants to destroy me. A year has gone already – how quickly time flies when you are having fun!

The treatment room at the London Clinic is in the basement. I was shown into a room with a large seat like a dentist's chair, the blinds were pulled right down and the air conditioning was arctic. I could see people's feet marching past above me and was reminded again of how little the world out there knew about the world down here. I have to admit that the surroundings were not particularly welcoming, unlike the staff who were just brilliant. First in was the lady from the catering department to offer tea, coffee, smoothies and all sorts. Then came two beautiful nurses who would be looking after me, Clare Cobbett and Ani Ransley. They are truly angels, and I value their friendship so highly. Much as the oncologist is brilliant, God-like even, these nurses are on the front line. They fill in the gaps and deal with all one's day-to-day fears and tears. Of which there would be many over the next few months.

The clinic is always busy and the nurses were kept on their toes all day long, going from one patient to the next, checking IVs and talking people through different aspects of their treatment. Clare took over and got me seated, taking my blood pressure and temperature. Then I was weighed: I had lost a little weight but nothing drastic.

'I am going to be the only cancer patient who puts on weight, you see!' I joked, hoping that I could lose a few pounds for the summer. Look for the positive I say. I was then set up in the very comfortable chair while Clare found my newly installed port and inserted the intravenous drip. There was a small prick, but he was only passing by with a tray. Sorry, that was an awful joke but I could not resist. It is being brought up on Carry On films I guess. This was now Carry On Cancer, 2013 style.

I was now effectively attached to the drip for six hours while various concoctions were fed into me. I felt very comfortable, and ordered a cappuccino and a Danish and read my book. To be honest it was all very pleasant and a welcome respite from my usual chaotic life. I dozed off from time to time, only to be awoken by the strident bleep of my machine announcing my bag was empty and it was time for the next onslaught.

The routine for my treatment is pretty much the same each fortnight. I arrive with my sample of wee and sit in this lovely chair which goes up and down and round and round and I am hooked up to my drip. This is where the wonderful port comes into its own, as they flush you out with something ready for the first cocktail. As far as I understand it, for my first twelve sessions I had three main drugs delivered through the drip from a bag. The one that has been consistent throughout this year is the unpronounceable fluorouracil, which comes in the form of a transparent rubber ball about the same size as a tennis ball. This sits very neatly into a blue purse on a belt which goes round the waist. The chemo is automatically fed from this ball into my system over the next forty-eight hours so I am free to go home. Come Sunday morning the ball had shrunk to nothing and a lovely BUPA nurse pays me a visit and takes out the needle and removes the remains of the ball, so that I am free once more. The extraordinary thing is that on chemo weekends I have so much energy because of the steroids, and I zip around like a mad thing. The downside is that it is difficult to sleep.

That first weekend was fantastic. I got up as soon as it was daylight and started cooking. The boys all came round for Sunday lunch and we watched Andy Murray win Wimbledon. What a triumph! Rather different from the following year as I write this. Let us not go there.

I was doing so well on this regime until about November. Then it stopped working, so Justin gave me a different set of goody bags which included Avastin which seemed to be the King or Queen of the IV-administered chemos. Another twelve sessions and things were still not improving. Then irinotecan was introduced and it seems to be quite harsh and I started to feel the side effects. I now feel very tired all the time and sick after meals. Meals? That is also a joke as my taste buds seem to have disappeared completely. Everything tastes like cardboard.

I have explained to Justin that the irinotecan is having an adverse effect and asked if there is anything else that I could have. I feel bad asking because the irritation is nothing in the great scheme of things. But it is important on a daily basis because if you are constantly battling sickness and generally feeling under the weather all your energy gets sapped away and I need that energy to keep me going. At the beginning of July 2014, I finally feel as though the illness is getting to me. The nurses were always asking me about the level of pain and asking if I had ulcers, numbness and sickness, etc., but actually I was not really suffering at all. I had managed to stave off the bad stuff longer than most, but now it is getting to me. But we are getting ahead of ourselves and we must go back to the beginning.

At that first session, I did feel tired as the day went on, but decided not to give in to a nap so I would sleep better that night. Afterwards I went for a walk round the block with my dear hubbie who was feeling a little melancholy. We talked a good deal about the future and what was going to happen.

I am not good at keeping things to myself. I can keep other people's secrets if need be, but my own emotions are a very different thing. I think of all those films where the star of the piece has an incurable disease and does not tell anyone and I'm not like that at all. When we arrived home from seeing Justin Stebbing that first time, my youngest son, Robert, and my stepson, Bradley, were home and I just blurted out, 'I've got cancer but the doctor says I am not going to die!'

Both boys burst into tears, as did Michael, and then me too. There was nothing one could say really. I pulled myself together and explained that I had these tumours in my colon and secondaries in my lungs and liver, but that hopefully with chemotherapy we could shrink the tumours and keep it all at bay. The boys wanted to know how long this would all take and of course we could not answer. Then my eldest son Michael came round and we had another heart to heart.

In a strange way I felt totally removed from the whole issue. It was not that I was in denial but it was as though I was talking about someone else. I became very calm and talked easily about the chemo. We even made jokes about it. In fact over the whole year one of the great things we have learned as a family is to keep a sense of humour. Sometimes one of the boys will come in from work moaning about a trivial event, like missing a bus or someone giving them a hard time, and I just look up and remark, 'Well that's nothing. I've got cancer!'

In fact, I was in Waitrose at the fish counter one day ordering some delights for the weekend, and there was a woman behind me who just kept tutting loudly every time I asked for something else. Then she demanded that they fetch another assistant as she couldn't stand there all day. 'I've got a bad back you know,' she announced grandly.

I turned to her and smiled, 'Well I've got cancer. So there!'

It's how I've come to learn to deal with things. However, that first weekend was bizarre. The sun was shining and everything in my home looked so lovely. To have my family round me helped keep me sane, but did not help me feel better. I had bloody cancer – how was I going to deal with it? And not just with the cancer itself, but with my poor family having to watch me day in and day out and not be able to do anything for me. Well I made a promise to myself that I would find a way, but when I went to bed on Sunday night I knew I was going to have to face reality. There were decisions to be made about the play I was due to start, and what would I tell everyone? There is a way in which when the big things in life have to be addressed somehow we are able to embrace them, but all the little things, the minutiae of life, really get to you.

As I lay there in the dark I listened to my heart beating and I promised myself I would fight to the end. There was so much I had left to do in this life, I could not afford to die. This new-found strength must be coming from the blast of FU2 I had coursing through my veins. What a great way to describe my feelings towards this bloody cancer!

2
PANTOLAND AND OTHER ADVENTURES

....

December 2011 and December 2012

I think it is time to press rewind for a while and fill you in on the rest of my life as it was unfolding and so, I am taking you back to when I entered the magical world of pantomime, I will wave my magic wand (pencil, mouse, call it what you will) and 'Bingo' we are now in Birmingham!

I had such a good time doing it in 2011 that I reprised my role in 2012 and it was during that time that I began to feel unwell. Looking back it seems so obvious that how I felt then was a sign of what was to come, but at the time I just dismissed it – as we so often do.

I don't know why I had never been in a panto, ever, in all my forty odd years as an actress. I did do something approaching a panto at the Pindar of Wakefield, a pub in King's Cross, hundreds of years ago. I was playing Robin Hood and dressed like Douglas Fairbanks Jr, complete with moustache. It was great fun and rather bawdy, as I recall, and I usually spent most of the performances warding off drunken advances from the audience. Well it was a pub after all, but it was also famous for its music hall performances and Christmas pantomime. I remember my opening song began, 'Give me some men who are stout-hearted men!' Need I say more?

We finished the first half of the latest tour of *Calendar Girls* in the first week of December 2011, and unlike many of my fellow actresses, who were off to rest or holiday or spend wonderful moments with their family round the Christmas tree, I decided to attempt my first panto playing the Fairy Godmother. What else? I was persuaded by the actress Kathryn Rooney who was in *Calendar Girls* with me. She is a very talented young lady, and a vintage performer in pantoland, and also the partner of one of the great producers of pantomime, Michael Harrison. He would also be directing *Cinderella*, in which I was to appear with the wonderful Brian Conley.

It was this cocktail of talent that persuaded me to dip my toe in the magic! I have always admired Brian Conley and remember meeting him years ago when he was first 'discovered'. Like many performers he was a non-stop showman. Nothing much had changed in the intervening years, and now, watching him rehearse as Buttons, I was so impressed by his professionalism and talent. Performing in a pantomime is probably the most exhausting job an actor can attempt, even more than a big musical, in a way, because at least in a musical there is a real story and each character can help move that story on. But in panto, the leading man or woman, that is the name in lights above the title, is never really allowed a break. It is relentless, and the audiences very much come to see their favourite stars, and demand 100 per cent. It is also an audience often made up of children, who do not sit quietly and attentively like they do at the Royal Shakespeare Company. They shout and scream and eat and drink and even run around. In some ways I was dreading it! However, it was a real challenge to me to make the little blighters sit up and pay attention, and my Fairy Godmother developed into a cross between nice grannie and grumpy headmistress!

We rehearsed in a dance studio in Fulham and my first day was so scary. The last time I had done anything vaguely musical was *West Side Story* at Coventry repertory theatre in 1971! I find dancers very intimidating. They all have such amazing bodies and seem to live in a parallel universe. Even when I was young and not too shabby myself, I would feel unattractive and lumpy next to these gazelles leaping backwards and forwards. Nothing has changed since then, and when I walked into the rehearsal room I was overwhelmed by the smell of sweat and perfume, deodorant and cigarettes. They all smoke like chimneys and eat junk food and still they look gorgeous. So I skulked into the room and sat in the corner practising my lines. We only had two weeks and I was still in *Calendar Girls* mode, up on a hillside covered in sunflowers. At least I didn't have to take my clothes off for this production. Mind you it might have been a show stopper, the Fairy Godmother naked on a swing!

Everyone was lovely and very friendly and I soon began to feel at ease and Brian, who I knew a little, was very welcoming and we were soon making awful jokes and getting on with the job in hand. I was taken aside at one point for a costume fitting and a wonderful wardrobe master called Tony Priestley took me in hand, literally, as I was measured for my harness to fly into the show. In the end, though, that all changed and I was instead placed on a huge moon covered in lots of sparkle which flew way above the audience and was very dramatic, but because I was seated I did not wear a harness. I held on for dear life with one hand with a safety strap round my wrist, and in the other I carried the biggest wand you could ever imagine. It was huge. Oh yes it was! It had hidden batteries inside the handle, and every time I went onstage I would switch it on and it would shine like a beacon. I loved it! I had a long white dress edged with ostrich feathers and a lot of sparkle sewn on the material. Tony was a master of sparkle and had worked with them all, from Mr Danny La Rue down.

We laughed so much during that show it was wonderful. Sat in the wings, surrounded by half-naked dancers, I would watch as the ugly sisters rushed off to do a quick change and I was at just the right height – or wrong height depending on your point of view – to watch the rubber falsies come on and off, and the jock straps, high heels and the harness they had to wear when they were flown in for the ballroom scene be put on. There was a lot of screaming in high voices I can tell you. It was magical and bizarre to see dancers bending down and doing ridiculously unnatural things with their legs while standing next to a Shetland pony, a real pony, who decided to have a pooh! Happy days.

The wings, essentially the sides of the stage, at the Birmingham Hippodrome are huge. It is like being in an aerodrome, but then they need to be to accommodate all that madness. The show opened with me flying through the air on my moon and introducing myself. There is always a technical rehearsal for whatever play or show one is doing, but for a show like this, with so much going on, it is probably the most important rehearsal ever. Needless to say it goes on for hours and, in this case, for at least two days.

Unfortunately some people take it less seriously than they should, and sneak off to the pub. Naming no names, but one of the men in charge of pulling the ropes to get me on must have had a few one night. It was very funny in some ways, but scary in others because I was a hundred feet up in the air. He pulled so hard on the ropes I was taken by surprise, and was only just able to grab the handle on the moon in time to stop me tipping off as I whizzed onto the stage, then stopped abruptly, then whizzed half way off again, then continued to the other side of the stage and then seemed to dive bomb down to the floor! I couldn't get off fast enough and spent the next twenty minutes trying to stop my legs from shaking. Still, all's well that ends well, and nothing happened again through all the eight weeks, and all those twice daily performances we did.

There was never any time for me to go back to my dressing room during a performance so I did sit in the corner every night. When I had accepted the job I had envisioned rather a cushy little number where I popped on at the beginning, the middle and end and spent the rest of the night eating chocolates and watching TV in my dressing room. No such luck, I was on and off the stage like a lady in those cuckoo clocks, which was a shame because I had worked hard to turn my dressing room into a Christmas grotto.

I always love to make my dressing room a home from home. I developed this habit while on tour with *Calendar Girls*. Wherever I was, in whatever town, I always liked to be within spitting distance of the theatre because it made me feel secure knowing I would always be able to make the show on time. There were times when we had to stay in hotels that were further away and then I would get very jittery, so I would often go into the theatre an hour or so earlier than I needed to and sit in my dressing room. You have no idea just how bad a state some of these dressing rooms are in, absolutely disgusting. Some theatre owners spend thousands on the front of house and never bother to make the dressing rooms habitable, so I always carried throws, cushions and table lamps and such to hide some of the more unseemly and grubby aspects of my living quarters. In the old days before ''elf and safety' we were allowed to burn candles, but that is all forbidden now of course. But I did buy a wonderful little fridge shaped like an egg and that just about held a bottle of wine and had room for my nibbles.

So I arrived in Birmingham with my usual paraphernalia and set up shop. However, being the festive season I needed a few extras. Straight to the font of all things useful, I went to John Lewis and bought a free-standing little deer that lit up and a very minimalist Christmas tree, which was a sort of twig with lights. I could not really have a real tree as it would be dead by the time we had got started. But this little twig was magic by the time I had hung it with chocolates and baubles. I popped out to the market in the Bullring whenever I had to fill in the time spent hanging around during rehearsals and I bought more and more rubbish! But I did create a wonderful grotto and all the dancers and the ugly sisters would come to me for a sweetie and a little Christmas cheer. The dressing rooms in Birmingham were a bit like offices, very grey and functional, so it was good to add the odd fairy light. I did have a TV which was great, though I never managed to watch anything all the way through as I was onstage half the time, but I got the gist!

Our company manager, Ian Sandy, was a truly extraordinary man and basically he held everything together. In any profession there are individuals who just stand out as shining examples of people who know their job. Ian was one such man. He listened to everyone's problems. He was the conduit between management and cast. This is always a tricky thing to do, as one has to earn the trust of the actors, while having a management take on things. Ian was perfect at everything. He died very young and very suddenly after I worked with him, and not only me but anyone who had known him or worked with him felt the loss. We did a tribute show for him at Birmingham in May 2013 and I was honoured to be asked to take part. Brian Conley, Joe Pasquale and Lesley Joseph and many more came together to present a great night's entertainment in Ian's memory.

I will never forget at the end of our season, like every year, Ian organised an awards show for the cast and crew. Nominations included Best Animal Performance, Best Newcomer, Most Embarrassing Moment: you get the kind of thing. It was a great night and the food and wine flowed. We all took the awards very seriously, and I was thrilled to be given Best Newcomer! I have the award on my dressing table as I write this. It is about the only award I have ever received as a matter of fact. But I promise you I am not bitter!

I seemed to have made a good account of myself because Qdos, the company owned by Michael Harrison and Nick Thomas, asked me to repeat my Fairy Godmother at the Alhambra Theatre in Bradford, with Billy Pearce as Buttons. Billy had played this theatre for fifteen years and is a legend in Bradford. I went up to promote the pantomime before we started rehearsing and met Billy and another new name to TV at the time, Brendan Sheerin, who presented a show on Channel Four called *Coach Trip*. I have to admit I was a little taken aback by the fact that Brendan was not an actor and I had never heard of him. Apologies Brendan. However, we had to ride round the centre of Bradford in a silver coach, and everywhere we turned people were calling his name and shaking his hand and I soon realised he was obviously very popular.

Pantoland is renowned for using TV names to win audiences and it does gall some of us who feel that it should be left to the professionals and not abused by sports stars and more recently reality show 'celebs'. It is hard enough for many actors to get work these days without having to deal with their jobs going to amateurs. In fact, during the seventies and early eighties, pantomime became just about the lowest form of entertainment you could get. Then thanks to people like Michael Harrison and Paul Elliott, who recognised the advantage of using professionals and keeping the tradition of panto going, things have slowly improved, and now (with the exception of a few, unmentionable productions) most pantos have managed to create a wonderful form of live entertainment again with a mixture of some 'celebs' but also professional entertainers like Brian Conley, Joe Pasquale and Billy Pearce.

As far as I was concerned I had to accept that producers needed to use current popular faces. In all fairness, Brendan proved a worthy contender for a regular place in the cast. He was terrific as Baron Hardup, and a genuinely decent bloke. God bless him!

It was strange playing the same part in a different place with a different cast. I was still on my moon and had my spot in the corner in the wings. In this production I had two lovely ugly sisters, Ben Stock and Brian Godfrey. Ooh did we laugh, my dears! In this production things were very much the same, but different, if you know what I mean. There were little Shetland ponies that still poohed all over the place, but no big horse as we had had with Brian. This time we had a huge dragon at one point, and one of the highlights of the show was Billy and myself and Brendan and Dandini, doing ridiculous things with props while singing the twelve days of Christmas. I will let you into a little secret here folks, with apologies to Billy, but the only trouble working with comics like Billy is they can be rather undisciplined. If the audience is laughing it is like watching an addict smoking or a gambler rolling the dice, they just can't stop. All well and good, but when one has done two shows in a day and your feet are killing you and you want to go to bed, you just don't need that person doing yet another funny gag. I sometimes felt like taking my wand and banging him over the head with it. What a horrible Fairy Godmother I am!

All in all it was fun and I managed, yet again, to avoid most disasters, except for one night in the forest. In one of the scenes the Fairy Godmother meets Cinderella in the forest and sets her a test to see if she is as lovely as everyone says she is. So I dress up in a ragged old cloak with my face hidden under the hood and presented myself as a poor old woman. Buttons, aka Billy, would also join us in the scene and spend the entire time taking the mickey out of me and making me laugh, which was all fine, and I could hide under my enormous cloak. I would enter the forest over a little bridge and there was always lots of dry ice, the stuff that makes the white mist, swirling around me. Well, I say swirling, but some nights the machine seemed to go off duty and hardly produce a puff never mind a swirl.

Then other nights, like this particular night, the stage was lost in a fog of thick white smoke. Nobody could see anything, least of all me who was trying to negotiate the steps of the little bridge while holding my cloak off the floor and handling my basket. Needless to say I missed the last step and fell arse over tit, which got a huge laugh so that was OK, and I recovered enough to finish the scene, but when I came off the stage it was clear I had twisted my ankle badly. By the second show I could not fit into my dainty fairy shoes. Talk about life mirroring art. Suddenly I was the ugly sister trying desperately to get my foot in the golden slipper.

But folks, all was not lost because I had another sort of golden slipper in my dressing room. Just before we had opened the show I had gone on one of my usual jaunts looking for festive material for my dressing room. I still had my deer and my stick tree, but I needed some more fairy lights and, as it happened, a pair of slippers to wear in the dressing room when I was pottering around, etc. I have to say Bradford is not overloaded with shoe shops, or indeed any kind of fashionable shops to be honest, but I came across a lovely old-fashioned shoe shop up a side street and in the window were a pair of gold mule-style slippers. They were perfect! So cut back to the dressing room the night of the sprained ankle, and there I was with my poor swollen foot but able to fit it into my golden mule. What a delight. They were quite fetching and rather added something to my performance making me a more dainty, old lady Fairy Godmother than the headmistress Fairy Godmother who sometimes crept out in my performance.

Michael and I spent a lovely Christmas in Bradford, which might sound odd, but we had a lovely time in our hotel The Great Victoria. Just like Birmingham, I had bought all sorts of delicious goodies for us to eat, including caviar and champagne. We had been very virtuous since a trip in October to Majorca to do a juicing course with an amazing lady called Deborah Morgan, who has written a great book called *Cut the Crap*. Every morning I used to juice fresh vegetables and fruit. But because I worked such odd hours it was difficult to know when to eat, so we would often just go back to the hotel and have a salad and a sandwich. We did make friends with the local Italian restaurant and on my days off we would eat lovely pasta and drink beautiful red wine. But I could never do that after a show late at night because it just gave me indigestion. We would also go to the cinema which was only across the way from the hotel and then to Frankie and Benny's.

New Year's Day we met up with Tony Priestley, the wonderful wardrobe master from Birmingham, Ann Smith, an actress who I worked with the year before in panto, and her husband Steve, and the ever lovely Brian Godfrey, and we had an enormous fry up. It was wonderful. Sometimes there is nothing better than a good old fry up.

So yes, despite the juicing, I was eating all the wrong things. Not my usual practice, but sometimes one has to adapt to one's surroundings and because I had such awkward hours it wasn't easy to eat at the right times. I had been quite ill on Christmas Eve, and Michael had taken me to A&E after our second show, which finished early, so we were able to drive straight to the hospital. I had been having really bad indigestion and then diarrhoea quite badly, and I was short of breath. We sat in casualty feeling very depressed. What a way to spend Christmas Eve, and I was exhausted as well, which didn't help matters. We finally saw a doctor who said it was probably nothing and to take Omeprazole for a couple of weeks. I did and everything seemed to clear up.

Except it wasn't just indigestion or a bit of a funny tummy, was it? When I was diagnosed with cancer Professor Justin Stebbing thought I had probably had the tumour for eighteen months. How strange it is now to know that it was growing in me then, and I had no idea. Ignorance is certainly not bliss and I want to weep as I write this now.

3
COUNTRY HOUSE SUNDAY

....

March 2013

When we returned from Bradford at the beginning of February, I went to the doctor immediately and arranged to have a stool test. That came back negative, so I popped more indigestion pills and thought no more about it. We had so much going on with a court case regarding Michael's business (of which more later), the Darren Richards' case, that it took all our time and attention. However, I was suddenly offered another unusual job, for me, in the shape of a new series about country homes.

It was to be called *Country House Sunday* and would feature some of Britain's stately piles. I jumped at the chance naturally. I have always loved going round stately houses, thanks to my mother's love of antiques and all things old and beautiful. Now I would get the chance not only to poke around but to meet the owners. I found this aspect a little daunting if I am completely honest. Would my Isme wardrobe match up to the job? How posh should my wellingtons be?!

Lynda Bellingham

Our British class system has confounded many a foreigner and one can see why, especially nowadays. Let's be honest, in the 1940s and 1950s, when one talked about the working classes there really was a working class. Nowadays we are nearly all working class, with a few very, very rich people at the top of the tree, and they are usually from another country. Our aristocracy still has the land but they don't have any cash – inheritance tax takes care of that! My dad used to say that an aristocrat and a peasant had no problem communicating, it was the man in the middle who caused the grief. I should just make it clear he was nearer the peasant end of the spectrum rather than the other way round! Once the Victorians came along and aspired to wealth and gentility, all hell broke loose in the social order of things.

I have met so many different people in my lifetime from so many different schools of life and believe me the most important things that count, in my opinion, are respect for another person and manners; just everyday thought for other people and the art of being courteous. There were many so called 'poor people' in society after the Second World War, but they still had manners. They didn't go round pinching things from each other, or fighting, or being generally angry that society owed them in some way. I am only mentioning all of this because, sadly, I think the aristocracy takes a good deal of flak from the rest of us and unfairly so. Their world has changed and gone, just the same as things have changed so much for everyone else. I was to find that meeting some of these families and learning about their history, which spans hundreds of years and is rich with the bravery of their ancestors who fought for our freedom, and then also seeing the struggle they face nowadays to hang on to their inheritance, made them very human and approachable.

So armed with thoughts like these, and with a great desire to see how the other half live, I set off with my crew to the deepest depths of Derbyshire to visit Renishaw Hall. As usual the weather decided to play dirty and, instead of the beginnings of spring and the odd hint of sunshine, on a March day it snowed! It was freezing and I had not brought any really cold weather clothing. I had a jacket or two, and a rain coat, but no scarves or gloves. Needless to say, my opening shots were in the garden knee deep in fresh white snow.

It looked absolutely gorgeous but after a couple of hours I was nearly in tears, I was so cold. We walked into the main entrance and there before me was a huge log fire and I ran towards it, and plonked myself down in front of it, while the crew set up the next shot. I was cold to my very bones and in no mood to make polite conversation with anyone, but suddenly I was introduced to the lady of the manor. Alexandra Hayward is the daughter of the late Sir Reresby and Lady Sitwell, of the famous Sitwell family. Sir Reresby was the nephew of Sir Osbert Sitwell, who was Edith Sitwell's brother. Alexandra takes her inheritance very seriously and is passionate about keeping the house and gardens up to scratch.

The Italianate gardens are just amazing and when we first encountered them covered in snow it was a bit like being in *The Shining*, getting stuck behind the long box hedges! Everywhere you go in the gardens there is something beautiful to look at, whether it is a statue or a pond full of frogs, or a secret fountain. When I was first introduced to Alexandra she was very polite, but cool, and kept her distance, but by the time we left a week later we were firm friends. She wrote me a beautiful letter when the news broke about my diagnosis which touched me deeply. I met Lady Sitwell, her mother, who though in the twilight of her years was still immaculately dressed, and I could tell by the cheek bones she must have been incredibly beautiful when she was young. Later in the week I found a painting of her and she looked amazing, and then one day Alexandra showed me some photos of her and she really did look like a Norman Parkinson model. Mother and daughter love dachshunds and when I had left I found a china mug with one on the front, and sent it to Alexandra saying 'Saw this and thought of you'.

What I loved about Renishaw Hall was the fact that not only did it hold all these wonderful priceless antiques, but because the family still lived in the house, it had all sorts of personal touches. There was even a statue in the main entrance on which someone had left a pair of reading glasses!

I was given a bedroom in which to change and it was all themed on the sea and seashells. There was even a chair made of seashells. It was quite exquisite. Goodness knows what the heating bill must be but in those few days, when it was so bitterly cold, the house was always warm. This is the problem for all these owners of stately piles; they cost a fortune to run, and so have to be made to support themselves. Alexandra works day and night thinking of new ways to present the house and grounds. There is a lovely café, run by a super couple who we filmed for the series – together we made a delicious gluten-free orange cake. There is also a fantastic vineyard which up until 1986 boasted the claim that it was the most northern vineyard in Europe. They produce a gorgeous Prosecco which, I believe, was sold in Waitrose. We spent a very jolly morning with me treading real grapes in a huge bowl.

I made two very dear friends in the housekeepers at Renishaw who were called Pat and Sheila. We did a bit about how on earth one would clean such a house. There were so many nooks and crannies and objets d'art to dust or drop. We spent a morning, me and the girls, climbing step ladders and cleaning the tops of the curtains, and then we skated round the unbelievably polished floors on our mop bottoms. They were just such lovely ladies and full of mischief, but completely dedicated to the house and to Alexandra, which was so lovely to see. The girls often text me and send me their best wishes for a speedy recovery. I wish!

There was also a fully equipped Victorian kitchen, where a lovely lady who was an expert on Victorian cooking showed me various specialities. Now that kitchen was bloody cold, and the cooking range was not functional, so there was no heat coming in anywhere. By the end of the day I was blue! I learned how to clean my teeth with a concoction of vinegar and baking soda and, as usual, I jumped in and tried it without thinking and it was disgusting. I couldn't taste anything after that. All the dishes like the rose jelly and the pies looked lovely but I am sorry to say that thanks to my earlier teeth-cleaning efforts, it all tasted pretty terrible. I can't believe I ruined such a gorgeous meal.

We filmed a similar thing at Ragley Hall, next in the series, only this time it was cooking with war rations. A lovely girl came to show me the joys of cooking without flour or sugar or eggs. There was absolutely no joy, and I cannot begin to understand what it must have been like to eat some of that stuff, although hunger is a great motivator, isn't it? I worked out, though, it would have been definitely better to live in the countryside where the hens were still laying and the rabbits were still breeding! It just makes you realise how lucky we are now to have such a rich choice available to us, and how ridiculously greedy we have become.

Perhaps the most interesting facts for me were to be found in the room at Renishaw with all the records dating back for hundreds of years. There were some fascinating letters from Edith Sitwell there. She had a running battle with D.H. Lawrence because she was convinced he had used Renishaw and her family members in *Lady Chatterley's Lover*. She was renowned for her scathing tongue and she uses it to great effect when discussing the merits of Lawrence's writing ability. I loved the idea of Lawrence's gamekeeper in the novel pacing the woods and making passionate love to Edith!

As I mentioned, after Renishaw Hall we travelled to Ragley Hall in Warwickshire. With all respect to Alexandra and her beautiful home it was the sublime to the ridiculous. This was stately with a capital S. As we drove up the very long drive, through fields of sheep dotted under unimaginably huge spreading chestnut and oak trees, the huge house beckoning us in the distance, it was like going back in time. Nothing had changed. I remember doing a book fair at Althorp, another incredibly beautiful house, and one of the perks of doing the fair, if you are lucky, is to stay for the night. Earl Spencer puts on a fantastic dinner and you spend the night in one of the many amazing rooms. Michael and I were put in the King William bedroom where allegedly his majesty William III spent the night. We were completely overwhelmed by the beauty and uniqueness of our surroundings. The wash basin and toilet were disguised behind one of the immaculately wall-papered walls which looked like a closet. As you looked out of the windows the scene was exactly as it would have been 300 years ago. Enormous trees, well of course they have grown a bit over time, and the odd sheep grazing on the sloping field. This was exactly what I was looking at now as we approached Ragley Hall. I got such a sense of time and history. Michael parked his Range Rover right outside the front door and proceeded to take photos of himself and his beloved car in front of his new house. What a poseur!

I met Lord and Lady Hertford in the stable yard. Henry is the 9th Marquess of Hertford and he is married to Beatriz, who is Brazilian, and they have four children. The house has a long and interesting history as you would expect, but by the 1940s it had been turned into a hospital for the war. By the time it was returned to the 8th Marquess it was in a terrible state, so the then Lord and Lady Hertford worked tirelessly through the early 1950s to restore the house and gardens to their former grandeur. The 8th Marquess is best known for the mural that adorns the south staircase walls. It took fourteen years to complete and everyone seems to be in it, all the family including the pets. I must confess it was not to my taste but what a great way of remembering your family history.

The present Lord Hertford has a fantastic collection of carriages which we filmed and then I did a piece with a supposed horse whisperer and a horse that Lady Hertford was worried about. It was a huge animal but I thought he was lovely. Maybe a bit naughty, but as we filmed I had the distinct feeling the whisperer should have been whispering louder! Anyway, what do I know?

The lady of the house was an absolute charmer and so full of life. It was hard to imagine how she had come to find herself in the heart of the English countryside, in this huge mansion that looked like Buckingham Palace. She basically fell in love, she laughed, when I asked her, and although she was homesick sometimes for the hot sun and bright colours of Brazil, there was always so much to do here on the estate she never really had the time to think about it. She talked so naturally about her children and how worried she was about their future and the future of the house. Her eldest son would eventually take over and, like any mother, her ladyship was concerned he would not meet the right sort of girl. Not that she was being snobby, far from it, but she was worried that the whole thing would fall apart.

It was really like talking about any mother and son, and I absolutely understood where she was coming from, I have the same worries for my two sons. It does seem sometimes that the balance between men and women has gone slightly skew-whiff. So many young women seem to chase the money and glory from a man but give nothing in return. If I married a rich man I would want to contribute in some way to the relationship, be it having a family or making him a good home from which to work – 'behind every successful man . . .' and all that. But a lot of modern girls can't cook and if they do have children they then dump them on a nanny while they go shopping! I do worry about it as a mother.

Being the owner of a stately home is as much a burden as a prize. The family live in a flat at the top of the house, which seems to me it was a bit like living over the shop! They do use some of the state rooms for special occasions but in the main, even though they own this sprawling grand house, they are closeted in a flat! Lord Hertford is also, unfortunately, not 100 per cent as he was injured in a riding accident, so he is often at home in front of the telly watching Australian soaps.

Michael was waiting for me to finish filming in the kitchen when Lady Hertford found him and dragged him off to have a glass of wine with them. 'Excuse Henry,' she told my husband, 'he won't talk to you when he is watching his favourite soap so we will sit and drink until it's finished.' Well Michael was very happy with that arrangement but he is the sort of man who is naturally curious and he could not help but ask his host about the estate. To the amazement of her ladyship, the two men engaged in a long conversation about farming and the like and the soap was forgotten!

I really admired Beatriz and how she had just taken the bull by the horns and made her life work in such different surroundings. It was very clear to me she loved her husband and family, and worked hard to keep her children's feet on the ground. She told me a wonderful story about a party they gave for one of their brood. As it was a special occasion – an eighteenth birthday I think – it was decided to use the ballroom. Believe me this was a *ballroom*. We filmed a Jane Austen scenario in it with a local Jane Austen dance group. There were about ten of us dancing a reel in the middle of the floor and the room was so vast that the ten of us looked like a tiny speck on the floor. Having been lovingly restored, I could not begin to imagine how any parent would open their lovely home to a horde of teenagers, never mind a listed ballroom with parquet flooring and gilded columns. Anyway, her ladyship explained that it was a formal gathering in the ballroom, a black tie affair, and there was a champagne fountain.

'But I know what these kids are like with alcohol,' she laughed, 'so I arranged with the wine merchant and the caterers to restrict the flow every now and then. I also spoke to my housekeeper and sent her out to buy lots of plastic buckets to put around the place so they could throw up as much as they liked but not on my beautiful floors or furniture.'

What a woman! Downstairs in the cellars they had created a disco for later and here the kids could change into dancing attire.

'I was shocked with all the girls,' confessed her ladyship. 'They didn't so much change their dresses as undress! They went from ballgowns to tiny pieces of material. I was very unhappy with these girls. They are supposed to be ladies.' It was good to think it happens to the best of folk, not just us struggling boring middle-class parents, who are trying to instil some measure of style into our children.

'I also tampered with the cocktails for this part of the evening,' said Beatriz with a cheeky grin. 'I had to pay full whack for the cocktails and the boy to mix them, but he was instructed to use only half of all the ingredients, which helped the sick factor considerably.'

I had such admiration for her and looking at all the family photos dotted around the house it was clear what a close family they are, which is no mean feat.

I loved the atmosphere of the house, and even though it was so huge you could still really inhabit a room and feel at home. Well, nearly!

Our last episodes were filmed down in Devon at Ugbrooke House, owned by Lord and Lady Clifford. They were both wonderfully mildly eccentric and what one kind of imagines a lord and lady should be like. This house was beautiful and probably the nearest thing to somewhere you could live in, supposing you found it in a terrible state and had loads of dosh to do it up. This house had been around in various incarnations for 900 years since the Domesday Book. Robert Adam was commissioned to remodel the house around the same time that Capability Brown was working on the garden. So there's pedigree for you. Alan Titchmarsh eat your heart out – mind you, I love Alan, he is such a lovely man.

All the rooms are just out of this world and interestingly used and lived in by the family. The place I loved the best was their private chapel. It was a gem and inside the house in the library there was a secret door in the panelling through which the family could sneak and take their seats up in the gallery, above the public and staff, and watch proceedings sometimes completely unnoticed by the folk downstairs. It was such a perfect place and we filmed the choir practising, their young voices soaring to the high domed ceiling. It was like a mini St Paul's. When I was diagnosed I received the loveliest postcard with a picture of Lady Clarissa and her beloved dogs wishing me better and telling me they were having special prayers said for me. I was very touched by this.

In fact I have to say that I constantly have to pinch myself when I receive such words of comfort, not just from friends but people I have never met. All their stories are a testament to bravery and courage in facing adversity. It is truly humbling and another reason I wanted to write the book as it is as much their story as mine.

The owners have a butler and wife team living at Ugbrooke. The wife does the cooking and he butlers. We did a great piece about setting a banqueting table. All the candelabras are absolutely in a straight line, and all the cutlery is laid using a kind of slide rule. The silver is polished to within an inch of its sparkling life and every glass looks like new. Each placement was a little soldier as I recall, or knight, so unique. I learned an extraordinary fact as we set that table. When laying the table should there be an odd number and if it is thirteen you still lay a place and go and fetch the witch. The butler actually popped off and came back with a rather large doll looking like a witch with a coned hat and horrible warts on its face and sat her down at the top of the table next to where his Lordship would sit.

'You are not serious,' I asked incredulously.

'Absolutely,' came the reply. 'Superstitions never leave us, do they, and this takes the spell of the number thirteen issue.'

Can you imagine going to this really posh dinner party surrounded by heads of state and sometimes royalty and you look down this beautiful table and see a witch rag doll sitting there staring at you? Adds a whole new element to *Come Dine with Me*. Mind you some of the competitors in that series look quite similar to the witch!

I discovered that Lord Clifford's pet love is his military collection and paintings of the Crimean War, in which his ancestors fought and some lost their lives. He was a joy to listen to because of all the stories he had to tell, and his obvious pride and delight in his family history. He also works incredibly hard on the estate to keep it up to scratch. The lands and garden have some very ancient trees and the tree surgeon told me all about how he goes round all year tending to them.

There was one stark reminder of nature, still standing tall and proud after being stripped of greenery by lightning. 'We like to keep it because it is as much a part of the landscape as its brothers, and is still useful to other wildlife.' Talking to men like that, who are just so into nature. Their complete love and dedication just makes one so grateful because without them we would lose so much of our heritage.

When we were there his lordship and his workers were dredging the lake, which lies at the bottom of a gorgeous sloping lawn. A painting depicting the same scene hundreds of years ago would have looked the same. But I did find a new spot to try something that may not have been around quite so long, but is delicious and should be kept going for posterity. A Devon cream tea! This lovely local lady does cream teas in her shop and makes everything and so much of it. She had a beautiful china cake stand piled with the biggest array of sandwiches you have ever seen. It was like a cream tea for a giant!

'Oh we don't like to stint our customers,' she said in her rounded Devon brogue. 'We never have any complaints. Now try one of my scones, and tell me, what is the correct way to eat your scone, cream first or jam?'

I knew this was a tricky question because in Cornwall they do it one way and Devon another but I couldn't remember which way round it was.

'Cream on first,' she pronounced, as I was just about to spread some jam across this enormous scone.

'Oh OK,' I murmured, salivating at the sight of the pot of clotted cream.

'Cream comes from our herd and I make all the jams myself,' she told me proudly.

Well I forgot I was going to be watched by millions as I spooned, nay heaped, my scone with cream and jam, and stuffed it into my mouth. I was just reaching a higher plane of existence in the joy department when I heard my director call out, 'OK, Lynda, close the scene please and make your goodbyes.'

She must be joking; I could not speak for five minutes!

I loved doing *Country House Sunday* and I so wish there had been another series, but sadly it was not to be. But, dear reader, if you want a lovely day out, search all these stately homes on the web and take your pick, they really are worth a visit.

Now back to the other story which is not quite so sunny I am afraid to say.

4
A PASSIONATE WOMAN

....

June–July 2013

The previous two years had been spent setting up my career again after four years on the road. I had loved every minute of *Calendar Girls* and although the touring was hard, and very tiring, Michael and I had made it our own sort of road trip. Looking back, timing had been everything. There was no way I could have spent so much time away from home and family if Michael had not been with me. Those four-and-a-half years gave me the confidence to push on towards the other ambitions I still had left in me but, more importantly, I realised just how happy I was to be in a loving relationship. I was killing the myth that sometimes lingered in my head that an artist or an actor has to live a tragic life of poverty in an attic to realise their talent.

I have seen so many marriages fall apart because the couple are not together enough, and Michael and I were never without each other in those four years. I don't know how we survived without a cross word, but we did. He was able to work from a laptop so had his own agenda and I spent a good deal of time doing work for the various charities I support. It was fantastic to get out of London and see how things really work in our society. We tend to think London is the centre of the universe, but it is only like every other capital city around the world. Oh yes it is diverse and multicultural, and exciting, but it is not remotely connected to the rest of the UK.

When I had finished touring *Calendar Girls*, I had to think about the next step for me. David Pugh and Dafydd Rogers were the producers of *Calendar Girls*, and David Pugh and I had discussed several times what I should do next. I did not want to go back to *Loose Women* as I felt I had no more to talk about. The problem with being on TV week in week out is that one runs out of stories about one's life; and the day-to-day stuff is not always thrilling and exciting and worth discussing. I also had the feeling that my career as an actress was not being taken very seriously. It is all very well having a high profile but if one is not careful these days you can become famous for being famous, which is not something I had ever wanted in my career. Television did not seem to beckon so I looked to the stage, and there was David one day, sitting in the alleyway outside Sheekey's restaurant in Covent Garden, which David uses as a second office, with a fantastic suggestion. He still owned the rights to *A Passionate Woman* by Kay Mellor. He had produced it in the West End nearly twenty years ago, starring that wonderful actress Stephanie Cole, and this would be the play to set me back on course. It is a brilliant piece of writing, a very dark comedy about a woman in her late fifties on the day her son is getting married. She is in a loveless marriage, and the thought of life stretching before her without her beloved son produces some surprising reactions from her, and everybody around her. I was so excited about this production.

I had an action-packed day when we auditioned five Polish actors to play opposite me. We already had Christopher Timothy onboard to play my husband, so that was great as we had been married before in *All Creatures Great and Small* and he is just so lovely. We had also auditioned for the role of my son and cast Peter McMillan, who gave a very impressive audition. The plot involves Betty, my character, having had a passionate affair, many years ago, with a young Polish immigrant who then gets shot and dies. During the course of the play he appears to Betty and brings back so many memories, not least how attracted she was to this very passionate young man. David Pugh decided he wanted a Polish actor who spoke English, rather than an English actor trying to speak with a Polish accent, so instructed the casting director, Sarah Bird, to come up with some names. Being the brilliant woman she is they duly arrived at Luton, by easyJet, one May morning. I then had the onerous task of spending a morning snogging five young handsome Polish actors. I didn't mention this to hubbie at the time!

Kay Mellor, who wrote the play and was to direct it, and David Pugh and Dafydd Rogers, the producers, all sat in the stalls and watched with great glee as I grappled with my would-be lovers. I can't remember whether Mateusz Demięcki came in second or third, but it was one of those theatrical moments where, when he opened his mouth to speak, we all just stopped and watched, completely caught up in his performance. He had learned the lines for the scenes instead of reading them, which is always very impressive, and he had no inhibitions at all – and just swept me up in his arms and made love to me there and then. Well of course when I say "made love to me" he was acting! But he was fantastic. After he had left the stage we all recovered our breath, especially me. I was having a hot flush, frankly!

David said we must see all the other actors before we made any decisions, and of course that is absolutely right. We did so and then we broke for lunch and went to sit at a table in the alleyway outside Sheekey's. There really was no contest and David rang Mateusz and told him to come back at two o'clock to go through the scenes again. All those other poor lads had all day to wander around until their flight back in the evening. Two o'clock duly arrived and we all trooped back into the theatre. I had had a glass of wine to fortify myself against another onslaught of passion. Who am I kidding? I couldn't wait! Sorry, hubbie, I'm only joking.

After we had gone through the scenes again David came up onto the stage and announced that Mateusz had got the job. The young man looked absolutely stunned and said, 'Please don't make joke with me. Is this candid camera?'

David was so excited. He told me later that one of his most favourite things in life is when he gets to tell someone they have got the job, which I thought was so lovely of him. We all went back to Sheekey's in the alley and had a glass of champagne to celebrate, and as we were sitting there a man came over and asked Mateusz for his autograph. They had a conversation in Polish and then the man left happily clutching his piece of paper.

'I am so sorry, Mateusz,' I said. 'Are you very famous in Poland?' It had not occurred to any of us, I don't think, that maybe this very talented young man had a great career in another country.

'No not really,' he replied modestly. 'I did a series for TV and everyone got to know me a little bit.'

A little bit?! It turns out he is the sort of David Tennant of Poland and his whole family is in the theatre. He works for their National Theatre and is feted wherever he goes. Not great news for our producers, who could see the wage bill rising in their mind's eye! But great news for the play and, as we waved goodbye at the end of the day and agreed we were all looking forward to the read through in a few weeks' time, I was on cloud nine.

The day of the read through did indeed arrive on 28 June 2013, a day I will never forget. I had been told there was a problem with a shadow on my liver that morning, and that I must cancel my holiday to Greece, starting that Sunday, and go and see a colon specialist on the Tuesday.

By the time I got to the read through I was in pieces. I told no one except dear Chris Timothy, who just gave me a big hug and said to try not to think about it until Tuesday. Just enjoy today. I took his advice and threw myself, heart and soul, into that read through. When we had done I was on such a high but as I gradually came down to earth while we sat celebrating the successful read through, I could no longer push the negative thoughts aside. Thank

God my wonderful, special husband came round the corner in the nick of time and whisked me away.

We decided to meet our dear friends Angie and John Chandler for lunch on the Saturday and we discussed the holiday that we had had to cancel. They had been intending to join us for the last week. It was not a very jolly lunch, I have to say, and by the end of the weekend Michael and I had run out of positive things to say to each other, we just wanted to get the meeting on Tuesday over with, and done and dusted. The day finally came and those unforgettable words resounded round the surgeon's office, 'Now about your cancer, Miss Bellingham,' and, well, you know the rest by now.

With *A Passionate Woman* I had finally found a project that was exciting and would set me off again on the road to acting glory! I joke, but believe me, acting is a very tough and cruel business to survive in, and I intended to survive to my dying day.

Yet now suddenly, ironically, I faced my dying day, and I was going to have to give up my dream. I was devastated when I realised that I would have to cancel the tour. The Monday after my first chemo I spent hours on the phone to my agent Sue Latimer. She also happens to be a dear friend, and so I could talk honestly and freely with her. David and Dafydd were prepared to postpone and wait to see how I got on with the chemo.

I asked my oncologist if there was any way I could have my chemo sessions at different hospitals around the country when I toured. Or maybe I could come back to London every fortnight and have the chemo on the Monday morning before travelling to my next theatre date. I was

Christmas 2011. This was the last Christmas we all had together
before I started doing Panto and it is the kind of Christmas I had wanted
in 2013 but I suffered a perforated colon which saw me in hospital instead.
I can now only hope we will have a big get together like this again this
coming Christmas, fingers crossed.

Flying in as the Fairy Godmother. 'Where's the bar?'

In my birthday suit on our wedding anniversary and my birthday.

Michael and me in Paradise in Pangkor Laut on the East coast.

'Yes that's right, Michael, you are King for a day!', in a procession in Tangjong Jara.

Both of these pictures were taken by Julie Phelan from Littlewoods/Very. She was brilliant to work with on the Isme campaign and I think both of these photos are fantastic. The fairy godmother picture was from an advert I did for Isme and Michael and I decided to use it as our Christmas card for 2012. Then Julie came to visit me during a chemo session and took the photo of me in the cold cap which is what you wear to stop hair loss during treatment. I love these two photos because the contrast echoes the Isme campaign's catch phrase I used 'This is me.'

My big day! A workshop for Calendar Girls, the musical, where
Mr Gary Barlow sang to me! From left to right: Tim Firth - the writer
of Calendar Girls, me, Gary and the gorgeous David Pugh.

The cast of the workshop that day at the Tricycle theatre in Kilburn,
11th July 2014.

Dressed as a 1940s version of a scrubber when I was doing Country House Sunday for ITV, at Ragley Hall no less!

'Can I interest you in a nice little doer-upper?' Michael's dream home at Ragley Hall.

Me and Batty during filming of Tasty Travels. 'A marriage made in heaven.'

'There's a moose loose aboot this hoose!'

I opened the National Centre for the Study and Prevention of Violence and Abuse on the 20 June 2014. Ruth Jones who is also in the photo was the lovely lady who approached me and we had had similar experiences of domestic violence. We both received an OBE.

My Fellowship was awarded to me by Lord Falkner at the University of Worcester.

From left to right: Dr. Kevin Pickess, University of Worcester Registrar; Ruth Jones OBE; Dr. Jan Quallington Head of the Institute of Health and Society at the University of Worcester; myself; Professor David Green Vice Chancellor University of Worcester; Lord Faulkner of Worcester and Professor Rosalind Foskett, Deputy Vice Chancellor University of Worcester.

Receiving my OBE from
Prince Charles on 14 March
2014. 'I could do with a
G and T couldn't you,
your Royal Highness?'

What a line up. It reminds me of the film *Kind
Hearts and Coronets* and I am playing Alistair Sim
as the head of the gang of robbers. I know that is
unkind, we all look gorgeous really. Left to right:
Brad, Michael, Michael, me and Robert.

Katie Mallalieu sharing my
award. Thank you Katie for
all your hard work.

clutching at straws and I knew it. Although I had no terrible side effects from the first chemo I was experiencing fatigue already, and flu-like symptoms which I tried to disguise with painkillers. It would be impossible to hold a performance together night after night.

The final nail in the coffin (if you will pardon the expression) was insurance. There was no way the producers would be able to insure me for a nationwide tour. So that was that. My career was to end, just like that. Oh I could maybe do the odd appearance in a TV drama. Or maybe some reality things and documentaries, but as to any more life-changing career roles?

Well it now seemed that I was destined to create my role as a cancer victim. The bloody disease had beaten me before I had even started. I cried my heart out. I know it must seem very odd to some people that I seemed more upset about my career than my family. Believe me, that was not the case, but the weird thing about death or the idea of leaving one's loved ones, is that somehow it's easier for the person with the problem. It is the thought of leaving them alone that is so awful. For them it is a terrible loss in their lives, but for me I would be off wherever, and out of it.

But in the meantime to live without working was just unbearable to me. I have been an actress for forty-five years. It has saved me from disaster so many times. I am defined by my work, in a way, as so many of us are in life. Yes, I have my sons, but they are grown men, and although I know they love me, they have their own lives to lead. My marriage to Michael has been so wonderful and such a surprise, and I am only too aware that I would be leaving him just as we were embarking on the twilight of our lives. We had so many plans to travel and enjoy ourselves. Michael also understood I needed to work as well. Everything was set up to move forward to a happy ending. But as we all know life is not like that.

I only found out my prognosis two days before the news was announced in the press. I had really had no time to digest my situation myself and, to be honest, I was still in a state of disbelief.

It is so hard to explain – although I wasn't in denial, I could not help but think there had been a mistake. I kept asking Justin Stebbing whether I would be able to cope with eight shows a week, and all the travelling. I think he too wanted it to be OK, so he never really gave me the definitive 'No' that had to come. David and Dafydd wanted me to take my time and make absolutely sure that I could not combine the play with the chemo sessions, but for them it was about the nuts and bolts of salvaging any funds, so they had to go to the insurance company which, in turn, left no option but to tell the press and the people who had already bought tickets that the deal was off.

Then the barrage of questions began. The main one being what kind of cancer did I have? I have been criticised by some people for not responding with the truth, but I was still in shock, and it was not my choice to put myself in the spotlight like that. The public and the press assume that all actors and everyone in show business court publicity as a matter of course, but that really is not the truth of the matter. I, personally, have always been wary of the press and for good reason. Many times they have tried to creep up on me, or my family, and I am often misquoted. I guess it is par for the course, and when I sign a contract for a job there is always a clause stating the actor must do a certain amount of PR. This I understand, but in general I would rather be left alone and judged on my work, not my social life. Nowadays the whole social media thing is a nightmare, and we are all tarred with the same brush. It is assumed that anyone in the public eye must expose themselves to minute scrutiny, and divulge every facet of their private life. Many 'celebrities' thrive on it. Well good luck to them, but that is not the answer for everyone, and certainly not me.

However, I have had enough experience of the media to know that if I did announce what sort of cancer I had there would be endless discussions about it, even if I was not present. Especially if I was not present. How many times have you seen someone on the sofa of a morning television programme who has been dragged in because they have similar symptoms to whoever is ill? Someone with the same cancer? There they are professing to have intimate knowledge of another person's illness. I did not want that, and anyway my body is my body, and why should I share everything with the world? So I declined to comment.

Then the attention turned to my hair colour. The papers made such a fuss about the fact I had gone grey, well white, when I appeared on *This Morning*. It was mad. I had tried to explain that the reason I had returned to my natural colour was because I had been hoping to do this play, *A Passionate Woman*, and wanted my hair to be grey and didn't want to wear a wig. Little good it did me. No one was interested in the truth! I spent the next month trying to come to terms with my situation. I was mortified that I had let down the two Davids and Kay Mellor. But they promised they would not do it without me, which made me feel a million dollars and gave me such inspiration to fight back.

However, it still left me with a gaping hole in my life and an uncertain future. Suddenly I was no longer in control of my life.

5
A TEXTBOOK CASE

....

July–September 2013

My new regime began in earnest. I was given various pills to take every day and lined them up on the kitchen counter. What a palaver. I had anti-sickness pills, painkillers, indigestion pills and the telltale sign of approaching age: blood pressure pills.

Without going into too much detail the one big problem I was facing was the bowels. Oh what joy to wait in anticipation for movement, then when it happened it was not exactly pleasant. Do not fear, dear reader, I will stop there but it is important to note that unfortunately, due to the nature of bowel cancer, there is a good deal of attention centred on things of that nature. One needs a sense of humour to get through it all and I want to be as honest as I can to get the message out there.

Justin Stebbing had explained to me that there would be side effects to the chemo which was something to look forward to. However, initially, through the first couple of weeks, things were not too bad.

Two days after chemo I have to take an injection for the white blood cells. I am pretty good with needles and such like, but couldn't quite bring myself to do the injection personally, so my dear husband took on the role. I must say he seemed to relish the job, which surprised me as, like most men, he can be such a wimp about needles when it comes to his turn.

The side effect of the injection, however, was three days of flu-like symptoms and I must say I felt pretty rough. It also made me feel a bit depressed about the whole bloody cancer business. As long as there is no obvious pain or signs of illness I could push all negative thoughts aside, but feeling grotty was not helpful. I even had hay fever. I mean, come on God, give me a break!

By the second session I had started to develop pins and needles in the tips of my fingers and toes. It was not unpleasant but distracting all the same. The skin on my hands and fingers was starting to peel and by the end of my third session I had no ridges to my fingers and the fingerprint recognition feature on my laptop no longer recognised me – I could have committed murder and left no evidence. How quickly one is forgotten. Never mind the public, even my appliances refused to acknowledge me.

The worst effect was that for a day after chemo, every time I swallowed it was as though I had a row of razor blades at the back of my throat slicing away at anything that came its way. It was agonising. The pain only lasted for a few seconds, but I would keep forgetting and take a sip of a drink, or something, and nearly hit the roof. There was also a problem now with cold things. If I took something from the fridge or freezer I got cold freeze burns.

This resulted in very strange looks in the supermarket as I would put on gloves on a boiling hot July day to pick up my frozen food from the cabinet. The air conditioning in these places is ridiculous at the best of times but now, for me, it was like a mission to the North Pole!

I was also suffering mouth ulcers, so had to gargle three times a day with salt water. My eyes started to weep and go all crusty, my nose would either bleed or drip at any random moment, and I was still having to monitor my bowel movements which became an art in itself. The pain-killers make you constipated so then you would have to take something to loosen the bowels, but then, after chemo, it would all run away with itself again and I would be back on the Imodium trying to slow it all down again. It was a never-ending saga. What makes me smile now is when people come up and whisper very solicitously to me, 'How's it going?' I feel like saying, 'Oh the cancer is great, thank you, but let me tell you about the chemo, mate.'

Then there was the question of my teeth. I had struggled for many years with teeth as I had wonderful strong teeth with no fillings but awful, crap gums which were not going to do the job of keeping my teeth in my head for much longer. I had had several procedures to cut away some of the gums and had learned the hard way about flossing to keep gums healthy. As a sixties child, society was great at dealing with the pill and sexual freedom, but it would seem dentistry had a long way to catch up with the beautiful people. By the time I finally summoned up the courage to get my teeth whitened it was all in vain, because thanks to the good old chemo I could no longer use the process as it is not on the list of recommended things to do.

The good news (oh thank God for that I hear you all breathe a sigh of relief) is with this particular chemo I was not going to lose my hair. I was rather fond of my new silver fox look so that was great news, and as work was difficult to get there was no point in pushing the networks for a starring role in the next season of *Breaking Bad*, though I must say I had rather fancied myself as an English Eccentric growing skunk out in the wilds of the desert. Me and Walt could have had a good thing going there.

Excuse my ramblings but the actress in me is never far away, which is why it is tough having to include all these unattractive physical aspects to my already ageing body. Getting old in itself is a difficult enough issue for any woman to face. I had been trying for a while to be positive and embrace the positive aspects of ageing, though they are few and far between. I went to see my gynaecologist, the most incredibly wonderful Marcus Setchell who has now become Sir Marcus Setchell having delivered Prince George. I have been looked after by him and his fantastic assistant Carole for many years, and was never really quite aware of just how important he was. I feel very honoured that he has kept me blooming with implants of HRT. I asked him if they would have to stop as well now that I was undergoing cancer treatment. The answer was absolutely not, which was a great relief because I was not sure I could also cope with the change of life at this point. Hot sweats *and* runny poo would be just too much to bear! I must say though that all these annoyances were minor in the great scheme of things. This was now literally about life or death, so a few ups and downs had to be tolerated.

One does become obsessed with oneself in a rather unattractive way. I soon learned to keep all my ablutions to myself for the sake of the rest of the family's sanity, but in a way it was also the only thing to do to feel I did have some control on my body. I hated taking all the medications and started to investigate alternatives.

I have two or three very dear friends who wrote to me with their suggestions for a natural approach to my diet, which was proving troublesome. I tried to eat healthily but so much food now tasted of absolutely nothing. Unfortunately the two things that never let me down in taste were salt and sugar, both the Devil's work. I was still following Deborah Morgan's instructions, following our week with her in Majorca the previous October, and Michael and I were on the juicing regime. I had also been advised that lemons were the ultimate fruit for cancer. The suggestion was to keep a bag of lemons in the freezer at all times and use the skins grated on food and in hot water and drinks as much as possible.

So my diet had become a regime of waking up with hot fresh lemon and honey. Then I made a juice for Michael and me of spinach, courgettes, ginger, celery and a couple of apples. It wasn't a great taste and it took me a while to get the ingredients just right. The temptation was to make fruit smoothies with strawberries and blueberries and all things sweet, but they should only be a treat as they are fructose which is another form of the dreaded sugar. The secret is to have fruit for sweetness, but always have a vegetable in there as well. I finally cracked it, and my best offerings are carrot, orange and fresh ginger or spinach, courgette and fresh pineapple, with ginger and celery and kiwi or fresh mango.

I discovered Ottolenghi cook books and boy did I go to town, especially after I received the most amazing hamper from my lovely gorgeous friend Linda Scott. I was having trouble sleeping so I would creep out to the kitchen in the middle of the night and cook these amazing dishes using lentils and beetroot and cauliflower. My cauliflower fritters became legendary. The whole family was put on this diet and bless them they indulged me. But they did enjoy most of it, I think, although every now and then I caught my stepson Bradley with a KFC or Domino pizza, and my son Robbie would disappear up the road to the Chinese. My lovely husband stuck with it but his meals were tempered with white wine. I do have the odd glass of red wine from time to time, with my oncologist's permission, but it is easy to succumb.

I absolutely became obsessed with cooking and would lie in bed dreaming up my meals for the week. It is amazing how running a household can take up so much time and my family do eat so much. Robert, Bradley and Michael often pop home just coincidentally around dinner time, and my dear husband only likes proper meals of meat and vegetables – no pasta or casseroles for him, thank you very much – which means I have to think of lots of meal variations. My sister, Jean, often joins us for Sunday lunch and my friend Pat and, of course, my grandson too. I now had my Tesco shopping online down to a fine art and my weekly walkabout round Waitrose for treats was great fun. Previously when I was working all shopping was done at a gallop like I was in my own version of *Supermarket Sweep*. Now I strolled round picking things up and reading all the labels. I bumped into Tom Wilkinson one morning doing exactly the same thing and couldn't resist suggesting to him it was a far cry from Hollywood where his very successful career had taken him.

He smiled and said, 'Ah, but Lynda, I get so homesick for North London and my Waitrose weekly wander.' And off he strolled happy as a sandboy.

Unfortunately for me I was starting to develop stomach cramps which nobody could explain. Then when I went in for my next chemo the nurse couldn't find my port to inject me. After much rather painful pressing and pulling it was announced the port had twisted over, a very unusual occurrence apparently, but Hello? It's me, isn't it? Her of the good fortune, not. So there was no chemo that day and I was admitted to the clinic to have another port put in. I didn't feel great about going back into hospital, I felt I had done enough of that now, thank you very much.

Lovely Professor Stebbing came to visit and told me some good news for a change. Every chemo day, before the treatment actually starts, the nurses check your blood and take blood tests to check your white and red blood cells. This then gives them an idea of how well the chemo is working at keeping the tumours at bay especially in the secondaries. If these markers go up it means the combination of drugs is not working and they will then try a different combination. Ultimately, the one sure way to find out what is going on is to have an MRI scan and after a series of chemos, usually a course of twelve, they will take a scan, check the state of play, and then either give the patient a break for a while or decide on a different cocktail. Apparently, the good news was that I was a textbook case, and responding to the chemo brilliantly.

We also talked about my food regime in relation to the stomach cramps and Justin reckoned it was not doing me any good so I made an appointment to see the clinic dietitian next time I was in the clinic.

The following week was tough. The stomach cramps were getting worse, and I was not sure what I should be eating, but as I was feeling sick most of the time food was not really my number one priority. But on Wednesday 11 September I had an MRI scan and the results were great. Cancer markers were down by 50 per cent and the tumour was visibly reduced. So onwards and upwards!

6
LOW TIDES AND HIGH TEA

....

The great thing for me during this period was that although I was no longer in the public eye much, and there was certainly no sign of offers flooding in, I discovered I had a different kind of life, and one I had missed out on so much while being away on tour. I also discovered with genuine surprise, and real joy, that I had so many people and fans who really cared about me. I have received over a thousand letters of encouragement and sympathy and they are just so amazing and uplifting. I was very aware when I started writing this book that I wanted it to be for everyone who has suffered or is suffering, not just cancer, but any potentially life-threatening illness. I am fortunate enough to tell my story like this because I have been in the public eye for many years, but through all the letters I read I learned so much about the human spirit and just how much people will go through to hang on to their lives and their families. It has been a salutary lesson.

It was also very interesting how many people assume, because I am a woman, that I have breast cancer. I am reminded of a story of a young woman who was suffering from bowel cancer and said she almost wished she had breast cancer because it got so much more press attention because somehow it was seen as sexier. She received a good deal of flak for those comments but I understand completely where she was coming from as bowel cancer is so difficult to talk about or present in an attractive way. Yet more people die of bowel cancer than they do from breast cancer, can you believe?

I am hoping to start campaigning for Justin Stebbing's charity Action Against Cancer, I have already worked with Macmillan Cancer Care in the past because my cousin was a Macmillan nurse, and I have done some work for Marie Curie Cancer Care as Jane Cotton, a charity worker I was close to, worked with them. It is only now that I have so much more knowledge of the whole set up that it has become clear to me that the most important, really the most vital, problem is raising money for research. That is the beginning and end of cracking these diseases.

So over the following months I spent a good deal of the days answering all these wonderful letters, many from the readers of *Yours* magazine for whom I write a fortnightly column. I also received mountains of flowers – some from people I had not seen for years. I could not believe that word can spread so fast. I could have adopted a serious and expensive habit of having fresh flowers every day in my flat. I loved it. The door would ring and there would be another bouquet. Thank you again to everyone for your kindness and generosity, you made an old woman very happy!

I had been starting to write my second novel, *The Boy I Love*, which is all about a band of actors in the early

1980s. It was due for delivery in October, but it was proving slightly more difficult than I had anticipated as I was not 100 per cent. My usual practice of getting up at five and writing until noon was a struggle. It was also apparent to me that I was writing a book which opens with a bright optimistic young actress setting out full of hope on her first job in the theatre. This was not my state of mind, and I had to keep reminding myself to be happy. Mind over matter again you see?

It was slowly coming together and helped by various outings away from home, like our visit to Bosham to see Mr and Mrs Albert Finney. A few years ago I appeared as a wicked widow in a series for ITV called *My Uncle Silas*, starring Albert Finney. I make no bones about my admiration for this amazing actor and I was so thrilled to get to work with him. He has two films that people will recognise him for: *Tom Jones*, a fantastic film made in 1963, and the second is a more recent one – James Bond fans will know him from his performance as Bond's oldest friend and guardian of the family home in Scotland in *Skyfall*. Of course he is one of our greatest British actors and he was first discovered from RADA in the 1960 film *Saturday Night and Sunday Morning*, but there have been so many since including *Erin Brockovich*, *Annie*, and a wonderful rendering of Hercule Poirot in *Murder on the Orient Express*. He is just a lovely man and his wife Pene is also gorgeous. She was a great friend of a mutual friend, Sally Bulloch, who was the entertainments manager at the glorious Athenaeum Hotel.

So I had rung Pene Finney and all but invited ourselves down to visit. They could not accommodate us as they had a dear friend visiting, who I also knew well from the old days, called Julian Holloway. Julian is the son of actor Stanley Holloway, and had moved to Los Angeles and had a successful career there. Julian and Albert were very old sparring partners, and ardent cricket fans, and according to Pene glued to the television coverage of the cricket, so she was delighted we could come and give her moral support.

She suggested we stay at The Richmond Arms in West Ashling. I rang immediately only to be disappointed. They could not do the Friday night but Saturday was free so we booked that and then for the Friday night, they suggested a B&B up the road to which they often referred their customers when they were busy. Having spent years of my early life in the theatre in B&Bs I was not overly keen but was persuaded to give it a try. Well it was like no other B&B I had ever been in. I guess I should have realised we were in the vicinity of Chichester as opposed to Blackpool. No offence Blackpool, but you offer a different kind of old world charm. This house on the water's edge was absolutely beautiful and Phillipa, our landlady, was so charming, and even offered to drive us to The Richmond Arms because we had booked a table for dinner there assuming the B&B might be a bit lacking. How wrong can you be? We had a lovely room with our own bathroom, and breakfast was a dream of fresh fruit and croissants and wonderful coffee all served in the garden in beautiful July sunshine. It was perfect.

Our dinner at The Richmond Arms was also wonderful. Situated in a tiny village with a pond, a pub, a fantastic village green and not much else, it was extraordinary to think how far people obviously travelled to partake of this amazing restaurant's food and drink. Albert told us he thought it was deserving of a Michelin star and we couldn't have agreed more. Outside they had an old French van which opened to serve wood fired pizzas so there were lots of happy families which created a great atmosphere all round, while inside the diners had the peace and quiet. It was the first time Michael and I had really had the time to sit and discuss our future, or fate, whichever way one looked at it. So we drank too much fantastic wine, and ate wonderful seafood and had a little cry, but soon the whole ambience won us over, and we relaxed. It was just like being in a small village in France or Italy. We took a cab back to our gorgeous digs and fell into bed and slept like babies.

After our superb breakfast we bade farewell to Pippy and John, our hosts at the B&B, and made our way to Emsworth. Pene had come to pick us up and gave us a guided tour. Albert and Pene have the perfect home within walking distance of the sea, and as Albi pointed out the town boasts over thirty pubs! Their house has a walled garden and herb patch, and it was full of gorgeous flowers. It had that wonderful calm about it which I always associate with walled gardens, as the old brickwork seems to absorb all outside noise except the birds and the bees. We sat and had a lovely glass of something cool and fizzy while awaiting the arrival of Julian Holloway. It was good to see him again and remember old times. We then adjourned to Albert's local, The Bluebell, and had a glorious boozy lunch. I had fish and chips, it was bliss. The two actors then went home to watch the cricket and Pene took us down to a little beach hidden at the end of an alleyway right opposite their house. We sat and ate ice creams. Michael and I left them at teatime and returned to The Richmond Arms which was to be our bed for the night. It only has two rooms but they are both delightful, so one really does have to book early to avoid disappointment. There was a free-standing bath by an open window so I sat in the water watching the birds wheeling overhead outside, and listened to the sound of doves, their gentle cooing interrupted by the harsh shriek of an occasional seagull. Another balmy night and this time we had our dinner outside and chatted to some of the locals who were very pleasant and welcoming. It really was perfect. The next morning we rose to a full English breakfast of outstanding proportions then set off back to London feeling at peace with the world. I know it is a cliché but once one has seen the horizon beckon it is a duty to take each day as it comes, and grab every opportunity to enjoy the hours and days you have left.

During these weeks though there were several pieces of sad news. My friend David Robb's wife Briony McRoberts committed suicide on the underground. One cannot begin to understand either her state of mind, or how poor David must feel. They had such a strong and happy marriage, which is unusual in our game. The funeral was a really moving and sensitive affair, and so many actors and friends turned out to wish her well which must have meant a great deal to David. I looked round the church and saw Samantha Bond, of Miss Moneypenny fame, sat next to Elaine Paige and Nickolas Grace. I bumped into so many mates like

Amanda Redman and her daughter Emily. Julian Fellowes, and his wife, and most of the cast of *Downton Abbey*, as David had been appearing in the series. I guess once again, though, for all the camaraderie in show business there is that horrible downside when you are not recognised for your work and it impacts on one's self-esteem and can destroy gentle souls. We also lost a good friend Ian, who worked with my best mate Pat Hay, who was the make-up designer on *New Tricks*. He was such a gentle and kind soul but riddled with cancer. Mel Smith also died on 19 July – another very sensitive and funny man.

But enough of this gloom and doom. On 22 July Kate Middleton presented the nation with the gorgeous Prince George. What a lovely big bouncy boy! I felt a bit closer to the action – if only a smidgeon – because we share Sir Marcus. In fact, later in the year Sir Marcus Setchell announced his retirement and there was a wonderful lunch in his honour and I was lucky enough to be invited. I arrived at the Hilton on my own, knowing no one, but thank goodness I bumped into Victoria Wood and we chatted away quite happily. I couldn't quite understand why there were so few guests in the room until the lovely Carole, Sir Marcus's assistant, explained we had been chosen as special guests to be introduced to the Duchess.

I then proceeded to completely mess my introduction up, because while we were waiting I saw Carole across the room and I knew she wanted to have her photo taken with us. I made a beeline for her, not even noticing who she was talking to, and even started to interrupt the conversation until I turned to the pretty girl to my left to apologise and realised it was Kate Middleton, and they were just about to have their photo taken with her. I was mortified and fled the room and hid in the toilet! When I came out I went straight to my table in the main dining room and waited for the arrival of the royal party and their special guests. I had missed my moment. Still I did get a lovely close-up look at the Duchess, and although I think she is too thin she is very lovely both to look at, and in her nature. So I think Will is a lucky man, as are we as a nation, to have a couple representing the country who are such a down-to-earth couple, but also who have a great deal of style and class. Please let our younger generations aspire to them, rather than being a celebrity style bling society who value nothing but too much money and no taste. Ooh, listen to me. But I can say things like this now, because I have got cancer!

July ended on a high note with tea at Claridge's with my sister Jean, a birthday present from a lovely friend, Katie Mallalieu. We met on Twitter, can you believe? She was a big fan of *Calendar Girls* but we have become good friends ever since. Jean and I stuffed everything in our mouths – in a ladylike way naturally – and toasted ourselves with a glass of champagne as we hoped it wasn't going to be our last supper! I was aware that this sort of diet was maybe not quite what I should be having but so far nothing else I had tried had worked, so I might as well indulge in a little something I'd enjoy for soon enough it would be back to the grindstone and my new routine of chemo, drugs and tests.

7
FIGHTING BACK

....

September 2013

I talked to the dietitian at the clinic and she put me straight
on a few things. Basically all my healthy cooking was
doing me no good at all! My particular form of colon
cancer cannot cope with too much strong raw food, such
as the spinach juicing, or the lemons. Fruit can be also
awkward because of pips in the system, and basically I
must revert to bland – and heavier – foods such as white
bread, pasta and dairy products. How bizarre is that?
Also, I was told, because the chemo takes so much out of
you, it is important to try and eat 3,000 calories a day to
fight the side effects of the treatment – 3,000!

I consider myself to be a little bit of a piggy when it
comes to food, and as someone who seems to be on a lifelong diet it had sometimes been a nightmare starving
myself of all the things I love. And suddenly here I was
being encouraged to eat full fat milk, cream and butter.
Mind you, I have always maintained that dairy produce,
as in animal fats, is so much better for you than anything

processed. I wish there was more education on food and especially where it comes from, so young people get a balanced idea of a healthy lifestyle, and more emphasis on the importance of eating proper meals too rather than snacking and grazing all day on rubbish. If you eat properly at mealtimes and sit and digest your food correctly you won't feel hungry. The whole sugar thing too is a minefield. When I was young cakes and sweets were a rare treat, not given endlessly as a way of shutting us up and keeping us quiet. We never had fizzy drinks in the house, it was water or nothing. I have always fed my children a balance of good and bad.

Anyway, I must stop digressing and get back to confessing to you that I am now, for the first time in my adult life, tucking into cream, bread and butter and all sorts of things I had previously tried to avoid. One of my happiest moments these days is to arrive at the bread counter in Waitrose at 8 a.m. and buy their fresh crusty loaf. I take it home and cut off two slices which I then spread with butter and top with honey. Accompanied by a cup of tea while reading a paper, and I have half an hour of sheer heaven. Of course even though my own dietary requirements have now changed to suit my own cancer, I remain an advocate of others staying healthy – not least in terms of finding the correct diet to stave off cancer in the first place. I think there is, of course, a great deal to be said for raw foods and less dairy. I would certainly say no to processed food, buy organic produce where possible and always source the provenance of your meat. I did hear an awful story recently from a guy who has been working with my husband on his current building development. He used to work in an abattoir, but in his last few years in that job he had been horrified at how many of the poor beasts that were slaughtered had tumours in their bodies; masses of them. Imagine if any of those rogue cells made it through to the meat we eat. Can they possibly weed out all the unfit carcasses or could some make it through into the food chain? At least if you eat meat from an animal that you know has been fed on grass that has not been sprayed rather than foodstuffs from their own kind, you are giving yourself a fair chance that you will be eating something that will do you good.

When I first discussed my cancer diet with another food fanatic who told me I must only eat raw food and never touch bread unless it was gluten free, I was almost in tears. Of all the things I had to put up with, the thought of life without toast and butter just about finished me off. Nowadays I practically live off toast. The other things I can eat are bananas and cereal with cold milk, topped with single cream and for supper, cauliflower cheese. Meat just tastes like cardboard, except I make a mean shepherd's pie which goes down well. Linguini with pesto sauce and parmesan cheese is another favourite. I do miss salads, especially when the weather is good, but raw tomatoes don't do me any favours and most vegetables irritate the bowel.

I had not been drinking alcohol very much but I checked again with the nurses. They are so lovely and I trust them with my life. 'Well, Lynda, you can have a glass of wine or two but not a bottle!' said Clare. Fair enough, but during August I did have several occasions when we had people come to visit and I probably overindulged. But, you know, I would suddenly catch myself thinking, why the hell don't

I eat what I enjoy? It is really not going to make any difference now and if ever there was a time for comfort eating it is now. However, my body immediately complained and I spend the next day in bed with cramps and sickness.

The one thing I have been enjoying is cooking for the boys and Michael. No matter how sick I feel, or sometimes I do not want to get up in the afternoon after a sleep, I make myself do it because I think these are the times you must not give in. Of course I rest if I have to, but giving myself goals and deadlines means that I can concentrate on them rather than on how I feel, and that way I don't give those blooming tumours a look-in.

The chemo was really starting to kick in, and the side effects had upped their ante. The pins and needles were ongoing and very annoying, and bizarrely the bottom of my feet – especially my heels – really hurt when I tried to stand up after sitting for a while. For the first couple of minutes as I started to move I was like a woman of 110! I managed to disguise this when I went out by standing and holding on to the back of my seat and feeling my feet touch the floor slowly. I waited a couple of minutes and then I would be able to walk away from the table fairly normally.

I now had thrush to contend with and the mouthwash the clinic had given me for it had stained my teeth. As I couldn't use whitening products anymore, I decided to put up with the thrush until I could find another way of dealing with it so that I could keep what white I had left on my teeth. The actress in me has remained vain enough to hold on to what I can!

My lovely friends and hairdressers, Tony and Andrea Schaverein, have continued to keep an eye on my hair. Not much Andrea can do with the colour now, but she gives it a glamorous boost with a kind of shampoo which stops the hair going that nicotine yellow colour in the sun. I didn't realise that even natural white hair like mine will do this after too long in the sun. Tony trims what is there. I have not lost my hair as such, but I now realise how blessed I was with very thick hair before, which has become very soft and cotton wool-like. But again I am lucky to have another wonderful friend, and very talented film hairdresser, Carol Hemming, who does my hair for photoshoots and the like, and she has taught me how to make it look thicker with products, and a marvellous little bottle of white powder called Nanogen, which she assures me is used by all the best film stars. I would tell you who but my lips are sealed!

I am telling you all this because, even in the face of something as all-consuming as cancer, I think it is important to hang on to your sense of self, men and women. During these early days before things got really bad I realised I was starting to change quite a lot physically and not all of it was to do with having cancer but actually with ageing. I have always said I wanted to age gracefully without Botox, fillers or face lifts, but the reality is harsh. My skin was starting to wrinkle across my arms and we all have our particular least favourite bits, don't you think? Well I had always hated the tops of my arms even when I was young but they were nothing now to the inside of my thighs! Lines on the skin pulling down the flesh. I would lie in the bath with my legs up, feet on the bottom of the bath and try and find a way to sit so that if and when we went on holiday I could get my legs out into the sunshine. I was beginning to hate this new old me!

If I had been feeling better in myself mentally I think it would have been easier, because I have always relied on humour and laughter rather than my looks to make me worth talking to. I have often said I would like to be the old bird in the corner telling amazing tales of life before an adoring audience of young men and women. But I was just feeling worn out and sick most of the time and that was not going to win me any listeners.

OK, I thought, more girding of the loins, Lynda, and let's approach the problem from another angle. I would give myself some pampering and spend a little money on some interesting attire and get away from the colour black, which I always go back to when I am feeling insecure. Because my hair colour had changed so enormously it meant I did need a few new colours to lift the tired skin. And would you believe it, along came a new and lovely friend to help me.

I live in a converted mental hospital (yes we have had all the jokes thank you, and yes, I am back where I belong!), and there is a spa in the basement of the gym here. Well I don't do gyms, that's for sure, but I do love a spa treatment and so now I popped along thinking it would be so great if this particular spa was good because it was on my doorstep, and lo and behold I discovered the most beautiful Brazilian woman called Christina. She is beautiful of soul as much as looks, I might say. She runs her spa with another lovely lady, also called Christina, which is a tad confusing but never mind. Well, between the two of them

I am nearly a new woman. Still old, but thanks to them I will probably be the best-looking corpse in the cemetery. I feel a little guilty about spending the money but hey if it helps me through the day it has to be better than a bottle of vodka. The manicures and pedicures really help the pins and needles, and my fingers and toes look pretty even if they are giving me grief. Christina massages my legs and now I can actually sleep through the night, and the facials she gives me have made my skin tingle and bloom rather than sag and pull me down. I do so recommend a bit of pampering, and your body will tell you how far to go with it. It is the same with the diet. Listen to your body and it will tell you what it likes or dislikes.

My tiredness levels were rising which was a real pain because I was fighting to get my novel written on time. My indigestion had come back too and, added to a lot of dizziness and sickness, I was starting to feel as though I was losing the battle. I called into the clinic and found lovely nurse Ani Ransley. She told me not to panic and increased the dosage on my indigestion pills. She said that when I came in for my next chemo we would discuss it with Justin Stebbing. I promptly felt much better and went out and bought two pairs of boots for the winter. Think positive, Bellingham!

Soon after that, I went to visit my brother-in-law in Hastings where we walked up a really steep hill and I did it without wheezing or being out of breath, which made me feel good. I continued to eat more carbs as the dietitian had recommended and I have to say the cramps came less often. I was learning to cope with the side effects of my treatment. But the pins and needles continued to be really annoying and on one particular day I couldn't hold my front door keys to get them in the lock which made me very frustrated. It served as a sign that I was ill, something I hated to be reminded of. If I was going to try and beat this, I couldn't think like I was ill, and I tried desperately hard not to dwell on it.

I was going to visit Crewe one weekend and I had to cancel because I felt so shaky. I was very upset as I had been so looking forward to going back to where I virtually began my career after a stint at Frinton Summer Theatre, which was a weekly repertory theatre. I had been nine months at Crewe and I have used the theatre there as the backdrop for the novel.

The trouble is not so much that I cannot deal with all these distractions, but if I go out anywhere and meet the public, or even my own friends, I feel the pressure to be 'up'. I don't want people to see me struggling because then they feel sorry for me, and the mood becomes downbeat when I am trying my hardest to keep things bright. Keeping bright requires energy, and energy is good for fighting back against all the negativity that those nasty cancer cells are trying to create in our bodies. Energy tells them to bugger off! I also did not want to feel paranoid about what I looked like. So far I had not seen any trace of that look that comes into people's eyes when they haven't seen you for a while and they are shocked at your slow decline.

As long as I had my hair I felt normal. Actually that is a lie because sometimes I felt absolutely terrible and hated the haunted look in my eyes. The pink patch of skin at the back of the scalp looked like a rat's arse. Tears would just spring up from nowhere and I would hate myself for giving in. These feelings came mostly at night, thank goodness, but I dreaded them descending upon me one day while out. I couldn't bear trying to catch my breath with a gasp of sheer unhappiness or feeling that awful lump you get in your throat when you are holding back the tears.

But the facts that were about to emerge were far worse than anything I had imagined in the middle of the night.

On 25 September, the cramps I had been experiencing won me over. I was doing a Christmas photo shoot for *Yours* magazine – they are that far ahead with scheduling these journals! We had rigged up a Christmas tree in my front room and I was going to be wearing something lovely and sparkly. I was getting into the festive spirit albeit some three months early. However, from first thing in the morning I had the beginnings of the cramps. I duly took my Buscopan which usually did the trick, and anyway I reckoned Doctor Theatre would kick in and help me through the day – after all, an old pro never cancels a job unless she is dead. Well, by four o'clock that afternoon I began to think I was going to die!

Once the team had left I fell into bed and decided to take a slurp of oral morphine that the clinic had given me for emergencies. I think I slurped too much which was a lesson learned: always do as it says on the label. By three o'clock that morning I was being violently sick. Thank God I was due at the clinic at 8.30 for my chemo, so Michael strapped me into the car and off we went.

It was one of those awful journeys where I just held on by the skin of my teeth trying not to be sick. Every bump in the road was agony. I made it to the steps of the clinic and ran to the loo and threw up. Thank God Ani and Clare were on hand to hear my tale of woe. My blood pressure was too high for them to start my chemo so they called the doctor on duty who took me through the events of the last few days. I just wanted to know what this awful pain was all about. Was I causing it by eating the wrong foods, or was it the chemo, or the cancer itself?

At this point Justin appeared and took one look at me and cancelled my chemo and admitted me immediately to hospital. Within half an hour I was hooked up to a drip feeding me potassium and zinc, then antibiotics to ward off any infection, but nothing for my stomach cramps, which were horrendous. I realise now that a good deal of the time the staff are given a remit by the specialist, or whomever, and they stick to that, anything else is disregarded. The problem for the patient who is feeling so ill is that one just does not have the strength to fight these battles half the time – it was taking all I had to cope with the cramps that continued to plague me.

Well, by Sunday I was so miserable with the pain I could not eat anything. I kept asking the nurses to please give me some Buscopan for the cramps as I knew it would help. Finally, thank the Lord, a super male nurse called Michael, always a lucky name for me, listened to what I had to say and went and got me Buscopan, which he administered intravenously. Within fifteen minutes I had relief. I do believe I have a very high pain level but even so I could not believe that patients were expected to put up with very obvious agonising pain. I hated my hubbie seeing me like this because I knew that it would make him panic. I tried to be as cheerful as I could and get through Sunday night and eventually Monday dawned and I was released back to the LOC and my lovely girls were waiting for me to continue with my chemo. We had to wait for my blood pressure to go down again and I filled them in on my pain adventure.

The doctor on duty came to visit and between the three of them they explained that the pain was being caused by the cancer trying to fight back against the chemo, so the therapy must have been doing something right at that time. They reminded me that in fact, despite my pains, the cancer had been reduced and the tumour in the colon was shrinking. I went home to continue my self-taught regime of pain management with a real feeling that I would crack this.

8
HIGH DAYS AND HOLIDAYS

....

I was determined to crack this and not let it rule my life. If someone had told me a year ago that I would not work as an actress for a year I think I would have keeled over and fallen off the twig. But here I am not acting but still getting out there and giving it some wellie. Over the years I have always tried to do as many different things as possible, be it for work or pleasure. Travelling has always been a favourite and I just wish I had done more of it. Obviously, my writing has saved my life and kept me positive. I have loved writing my second novel *The Boy I Love* which is due out in January 2015. I apologise for the plug but ignorance is not bliss, you need to know about my efforts! And I was delighted to be asked to do this book too which has seen me up at 5 a.m. in the morning tip tapping away.

At least I can say I am not working as an actress because I have been fighting off cancer, rather than having had to reach a point in my career where nobody wants me because of my age. Age is a problem. There are too many of us now who are reaching, or have reached, their golden sixties, and there are just not enough roles to go round. I used to think that if I could just keep going until I was in my sixties all the competition would have fallen by the wayside and it would just be me and Miss Marple. Looking back over this year I have been able to distance myself from that old world and managed, I hope, to get a less impassioned view of my world.

It has always been complicated in that in the old days the theatre was regarded as so much more important than TV or films, and there is a residue of that attitude, I think. When I did the Oxo commercials in the eighties and nineties there were several directors and casting directors who would never even bother to see me because I was regarded as a TV personality. Well, how that has all changed in the last ten years. There is hardly anything on television that does not feature a 'personality' or the new buzz word 'celebrity', how I hate it. It is an insult to all the hardworking actors out there who used to be the mainstay of television. It is all about the face of the moment, even if it only lasts five minutes. When I watch Alibi or Gold there are so many wonderful actors to watch, and not just as the star of a show. The supporting roles were always filled with wonderful characters we all knew and trusted too.

Interestingly, this divide also used to happen between film and television actors too. More so in America where you would hear a film actor (out of work naturally) announce grandly, 'Oh my God I would never do episodic – it would ruin my film career!' Episodic refers to any kind of TV serial. As I say, they usually were working as a waiter or waitress at the time. But that has all changed in the last few years and now American TV produces some of the best drama in the world. But where is the UK in all this?

Still filling three-quarters of screen time with 'celebrities' in reality shows, because it is easy and cheap. It breaks my heart. Of course there is room for reality shows, but constant, non-stop wall-to-wall moving wallpaper?

I was asked to present an award at the Olivier Awards 2013 in the West End. These are the awards for Theatreland, so I was very chuffed to think I was still considered worthy of mixing with the proper actors. When I was doing panto in Bradford, that winter, I became close to the lovely actors playing the ugly sisters. Well, I already knew Brian Godfrey but not Ben Stock, who is a super young actor. One evening a whole gang of Ben's friends came to the show and I met a guy called Julian Bird, who is the chief executive of the Society of London Theatre and Theatrical Management Association and runs the Olivier Awards.

'How fortuitous to meet you, Lynda. We would love to invite you to present an award for us if you would consider it?'

'Would I? Not half!'

The gong was for best male performance in a musical which was to be awarded to Michael Ball in *Sweeney Todd*, no less. I knew Michael so that was an added bonus, and the cherry on the cake was I would present the award with Brian May who I know because his wife, Anita Dobson, who needs no introduction from me, took over from me in *Calendar Girls*.

I was so nervous as the night drew closer, and was encouraged to hear that Brian was also having stage fright. When we met up on the night we had very cleverly managed, without intending to, to colour co-ordinate ourselves into black and white, and though I say so myself I thought we looked rather smart!

I had such a good evening because I didn't care what anybody thought of me or whether I had a job to match those of the fine actors and actresses who surrounded me because actually I did have a fantastic job to go into, which was *A Passionate Woman*, and at that time I couldn't wait to show the world what I could do.

I always felt that *Calendar Girls* did not get the appreciation it deserved because it was such a commercial success. Once again we hit the snob button because some people seem to think that making money is not the 'done thing'. It is considered better to appear in a financial flop that is 'true drama, dear', than a play that played to full houses for four years and drew standing ovations!

I was thrilled to be made privy to the plans to turn the play into a musical. David Pugh told me that they were working with the original creator of *Calendar Girls*, the writer Tim Firth, on the project and I thought it was a terrific idea. Sure enough the work has been progressing and at the beginning of July 2014 David rang and asked me if I would like to hear a couple of songs from the show that Tim and Gary had written. One of them was entitled 'To My Russian Friend' and it sees my original character, Chris, singing to a bottle of vodka. Not wanting to appear ignorant and ask, 'Who the hell is Gary?' I trotted along to a studio in North London somewhere, and waited to be enlightened. Boy, was I enlightened! In through the door came Gary Barlow who sat down at the piano and sang to me! Me, little old lady with a stoma bag, being serenaded by Gary Barlow. All I can say is Take That and shove it up your jumper, Mrs.

It was brilliant, absolutely wonderful, and a week later I watched a workshop with tears rolling down my face, it was so moving and the cast were all perfect. I know I must sound so theatrical and lovey-like, but sometimes, folks, you see something being created, and it is so inspiring, and it makes me realise how lucky I am to do something I still love so much. For all the bullshit in the business, there are also incredible moments of brilliance and teamwork, and lifelong friendships made.

Talking of lifelong friends, my bridesmaid three times over, and lovely friend Lynda La Plante, was recently interviewed about her new book and she also talked about a play she has written which will go into production next year. It is called *Murder Weekend* and stars Elaine Paige, Christopher Biggins, Lesley Joseph and me. She had already mentioned it to me but I explained that I would probably have to be ruled out because no one would insure me with cancer. 'I will pay for your insurance, Bellic.' (That is my nickname by the way, rather apt bearing in mind my stomach problems. Oh the irony.) Bless her cotton socks for that kind of loyalty. Friendships have always been important to me but never more so than now I was going through something so daunting as cancer treatment.

Another dear friend is Helen Worth, of *Corrie* fame. Here is another very talented actress and to my great delight she got married on 6 April 2013 at St James's in Piccadilly, with a fantastic reception at The Ritz, no less. It was a wonderful day, though dare I whisper, full of traps, because I absolutely did not want to call any of the *Corrie* actors by their character names – which is so easy to do when you become so familiar with their characters and the world they create in these programmes, but a heinous sin in my book. After a couple of glasses of champagne I had to keep stopping for a second before I introduced anyone to anyone and re-run their names through my head! It was a nightmare. Helen had been on her own far too long in my opinion, so it was jolly good to see her snapped up by the handsome, and very talented music teacher and choir master, Mr Trevor Dawson. Take a bow, sir, and congratulations to them both.

With so much of my time now taken up with my treatment, I was over the moon to receive another lovely invitation in April 2014 to present an award at the British Craft Awards. So I am not completely forgotten, I thought to myself. I am a great supporter of the production team on any television show or film. For years they were sort of treated like second-class citizens. The big boys – the cinematographers and art director and the like – get all the attention in the spotlight but the guys making the props, the wardrobe lady sewing the hems and the hair and make-up girls and boys who have to wrestle with a smelly, still drunk, actor or film star at five in the morning should be acknowledged too. I was therefore thrilled to be involved in this ceremony to honour their talents.

One of the decisions Michael and I made when we got married was that we would make time to travel. We both loved the same kind of places and the same luxury! We are not campers or walkers I am afraid, we love luxury and retreats. This can make the holiday rather expensive so my husband is often on the laptop for days scanning possible bargains. We have been very lucky sometimes and because of a job I can manage to wrangle a deal, though I hate those people who spend their entire lives trying to get everything for nothing.

In May 2012 we set off for Malaysia. Having finished the final tour of *Calendar Girls*, and wrestled with our court case, we were in dire need of peace and quiet. Thanks to a lovely lady called Kathryn Peel who has a PR company called Ophir, which deals in luxury travel, we booked to go to two different spa resorts. The first was on the east coast of Malaysia and called Tanjong Jara. The second spa was on a small island off the west coast of the mainland called Pangkor Laut, which we went to afterwards. Both were part of a group owned by a Chinese company called YTL and we were so impressed with their whole ethos.

Tanjong Jara was wilder and more natural than Pangkor Laut. Hidden up a long drive in thick leafy vegetation, with the usual wood and rattan villas, there were beautifully laid out paths down to the sea and round the resort. There was a hidden oasis where a discreet bar by a pool could be found and there were tall palm trees swaying above us. One could walk along a practically deserted beach, as the waves crashed onto the shore, and imagine life on a desert island. We were very lucky to be upgraded to a beach front villa. I was primarily there to write my first novel *Tell Me Tomorrow*. I had just under three weeks to break the back of the manuscript, so time was precious. We made a plan where I would rise really early, before the sun rose in fact, and start on the laptop. I would sit on the veranda of the villa and watch the sun rise, and the birds dip and dive above and, most exciting of all, the arrival of the large monitor lizards waddling along the seashore, their huge tales flicking sand behind them. It was like being in a Hemingway novel writing my own novel. Sometimes when I couldn't write and I gazed out to sea, desperate for inspiration, my eye would be caught by the activities of a huge spider weaving a web just above my head. I did not find that quite so inspiring, though, and would leap up and flap it away. What a wuss!

Michael and I would walk across to the restaurant and have breakfast together and then he would take off up the beach until he was no more than a pink speck on the horizon. He loves to wear pink shirts so he was always easy to spot. I would try to write until at least two in the afternoon and then allow myself some sunbathing and a snooze. We ate dinner really early, which was always delicious, and I became addicted to cream coconut prawns.

We would return to our villa and climb into this impossibly huge bed and watch English TV on the laptop, because Michael had this ingenious device called a Slingbox. I know it must sound so unimaginative to some of you but watching TV is the way Michael falls asleep while I read. However, it is sometimes difficult to concentrate on a book when you are writing one at the same time so I was able to succumb to the joys of *Coronation Street* from afar.

There were some wonderful moments while we were there, especially when we were given the lovers' welcome by the locals. You are King and Queen for the day. Every breakfast time Michael and I had watched with glee as poor unsuspecting couples were being covered with garlands of flowers and walked round the gardens with funny hats on. It was great fun really, but very loud, with loads of chanting and drum banging. One morning as we were chomping our way through a gorgeous pile of fresh fruit, we remarked on the approaching band and laughed to ourselves as we looked around for today's recipients of the flower power. Oh dear, they were marching determinedly towards our table. Michael tried to get up and leave but it was too late. A hand on the shoulder and he was back in his seat covered in an array of foliage which actually, I must say, matched his pink shirt perfectly. Talk about colour coordinated. In a flash we were transformed into a cross between amiable pirates, with our printed scarves, and tribal warriors with our flowers and spears. Off we went to the cheers of the rest of the guests (you wait, I thought), round and round the garden, under and over ponds and streams, until we reached the ultimate destination, which was a fountain where we were doused liberally in water. Oh joy!

Part of being the King and Queen for the day also involved an amazing massage in the spa. We were put in a bath under a kind of awning and washed. The water was very green but smelled wonderful! We were then led, wrapped in our cotton wraps of many colours, to a room full of light with two beds next to each other. We were made to lie down and we each had a gorgeous handmaiden who proceeded to scrub us, oil us, pound us and moisturise us. I felt like a piece of fillet steak! We both tried to make conversation but as the session went on we both drifted into the wonderful world of sleep. Michael insisted I woke him with my snoring and I retaliated with the same accusation. We both snored according to our lovely girls who found all our squabbling hilarious. Having had our massage we were then taken back to the bath in the garden and left to sit in water full of flower petals until I began to feel a little wrinkled. I did not want to rise up from the water resembling an ugly fruit!

We were then left to dry ourselves and given fresh wraps. We left the spa after three hours of pampering and wandered back to our villa in a haze of sweet smelling oils. I think we virtually passed out that night we were so relaxed.

After ten days we left Tanjong Jara and drove back to Kuala Lumpur where we took a plane to the west of the island, and then another drive to the coast where we boarded a motor launch to take us to Pangkor Laut. It was very hot, and all this travelling was not ideal, but YTL, the company who ran the whole organisation, just had it down pat. Every detail was perfect. The car was spacious and air conditioned with water ready for our consumption.

We arrived at the landing stage and checked in, so the spa would know we would be arriving soon. A lovely air-conditioned waiting room with a cooling cocktail greeted us as we waited for our luggage to be loaded onto the motor launch, and the ride itself across the bay was exhilarating with the wind in our hair and the dramatic coastline of Malaysia in our sights. As we approached the island the huge trees and palms towered over us and the hills filled the sky, it was very impressive. The boat arrived at a long jetty and we followed the porter towards a beautiful, almost colonial-style porch and front desk. Acres of marble floors, huge pillars and enormous white sofas were the order of the day. There were no walls so there was a soft breeze lifting the voile drapes and whispering in the foliage that adorned huge plant pots. I was in heaven.

We were greeted by a beautiful young lady, immaculately dressed in a linen suit, who spoke perfect English. After all of our details had been taken she took us through a few of the amenities, none of which I could remember afterwards – I always find that happens, and wonder, am I the only guest who nods inanely as the receptionist carefully explains what is on offer? Anyway there was plenty of time for us to discover the delights of the island for ourselves later.

We were escorted to a buggy and driven to a jetty further down the beach. We then walked across the wooden walkway, with the sparkling turquoise sea below us, towards our villa which was rising out of the water to greet us. The porter opened the door and I just gasped, it was so perfect. There was a huge bedroom with a door leading onto a veranda looking out to sea and the islands beyond. The bathroom had a huge bath by a window which opened to the sea and everything was rattan or bamboo with rather beautiful wood furniture in the bedroom. The bed was huge and covered in flowers and there was a welcome note addressed to Michael and Lynda which was a nice touch and a clever sell too, don't you think? Everywhere we went in the hotel and spa the staff always greeted us by our first names. The very first morning as we walked to breakfast staff smiled and waved saying,

'Good morning, Lynda and Michael.'

'How do they know our names?' I whispered to Michael over breakfast.

We asked one of the waiters who laughed and replied, 'When you arrive at the boat house to take the launch we take your photo and then you are pinned on a wall and every day the staff have to study the photos and learn all the names of the guests.' I think that is incredibly impressive if not a little scary!

We quickly fell into the old routine from the first part of our holiday and I would rise early and write for a couple of hours then Michael and I would walk to the restaurant. The restaurant was a lovely stroll along the walkway then through some of the gardens, and finally we would arrive at the main restaurant which served absolutely everything you could possibly imagine and from every corner of the earth. Chinese breakfast specialities such as boiled fish and noodles stood alongside porridge and cream, or a full English fry up, it was fascinating. I would then return to the villa to write and Michael would set off to the spa. He would return a few hours later smelling like a curry, wrapped in a tie-dyed sarong, looking as if he had been smoking something naughty because he was not on the planet, he was so relaxed!

I loved every day spent there. We ate sushi some nights, and there was an incredible Chinese restaurant built in a tree which served food like I have never tasted before. Our wedding anniversary and my birthday arrived and our bed was covered in garlands and good wishes. We had a beach dinner on the sea shore watching the sun go down, and then we walked back in the moonlight. The moon was so huge and so bright which was just as well, as we suddenly encountered an enormous monitor lizard on our walk way. He looked at us, and we looked at him, and nobody moved. I shushed him rather pathetically and he started towards us.

'Help!' I squeaked. 'Michael, do something.'

'Like what,' whispered my beloved. 'He is bloody enormous!' And he was about twelve foot long, like a small dragon, and not friendly.

We must have looked so pathetic standing there in the moonlight in our glad rags, waving our arms about. Fortunately they have members of the staff patrolling at night and a very nice young man came and moved the lizard on. It waddled away and slipped into the water silently. Phew!

It was the most memorable holiday because I used all the emotions I went through in that beautiful place in *Tell Me Tomorrow*. The holiday also served as a reminder of how lucky I was to get another crack at a relationship aged sixty, which is when Michael married me. We have actually been together now for ten years this November and I have never known time go by so fast. Sometimes during these last few months I have marvelled at how deceptive time can be. A minute can last for hours and an hour passes in a minute. I have tried to grasp each moment and savour it because, although it is such a cliché, it is so true that we just do not appreciate what we have, and we must learn – I must learn – to live in the moment, especially now that I know my time is limited.

In a way living in the moment is what one does on a holiday, I think. We take these precious moments and keep them close, often capturing them in a photo or a film, but for me it is keeping them in my heart that really counts. Writing now about Pangkor Laut, I can smell the flowers in the room and taste the sushi on my tongue, it is so vivid to me.

The other holiday we have had more recently was a trip to Lake Como. I am a huge fan of George Clooney and we were joking one day about how wonderful it would be if, as part of my bucket list, I could visit Lake Como and bump into George and persuade him to let me play a cameo role in one of his films. I would even be happy with a non-speaking part in a Nespresso commercial if I could sit on his lap! I do not have a bucket list as it happens, as I am too busy enjoying what is around me, but still it prompted us to get out and do something and we booked to go to Lake Como.

I love reading travel brochures and will always manage to find the most glamorous, and usually most expensive, locations in the world. Como was no exception. I knew there was an incredible hotel on the edge of the lake called the Villa d'Este.

'Just ring and see how much it is,' I said to Michael, as we were surfing the net for a hotel.

'I already have,' he replied with a sigh. 'It is fifteen hundred euros a night without breakfast.'

'Oh that is outrageous,' I exclaimed. 'No breakfast? We can't possibly go there!'

I love to dream, but we did find a beautiful hotel in Bellagio called The Belvedere which was like a sort of baby cousin to the Villa d'Este, with sloping lawns down to a lovely pool and garden rooms with balconies looking across the lake. Sadly, they had all gone and we could only get a room at the back, but it didn't matter though, we made the best of it, and it was a very pleasant hotel and the staff were fantastic.

We would walk ten minutes into Bellagio and be transported back hundreds of years. The buildings were painted in all those wonderful Mediterranean colours of ochre and bull's blood. The tiny church with its solitary bell chimed across the rooftops. It was heaven. The first shop we hit as we walked into the town was a *pasticerria* and the smell of fresh pastries filled with almond paste and coated in vanilla powder was out of this world. My dream was always to have a place eventually in Italy or the South of France, where I could sit outside and people watch. Mornings would be a cappuccino and a pastry, and afternoon, or early evening, would be a glass of wine and toasted almonds. Not much to ask is it really?

So every day we would walk into the town, stopping for a coffee and pastry and then continue down the narrowest cobbled streets, filled to bursting with the most gorgeous shops imaginable. Oh dear, it was torture for me. I could have spent thousands of pounds on jewellery, bags and shoes and paintings and all sorts. Michael wouldn't let me go into town on my own! One day we were in one of these amazing boutiques and the beautiful Italian lady who was serving me asked me if I was famous.

'Not really,' I said, 'Though I am quite well known on the TV in England.'

She was very excited because one of her customers, who was English, had recognised me and told her I was an actress. They love actresses in Italy, they are like royalty.

Well, I became a local celebrity because she then told the lady in the cake shop who told the man in the pizzeria and suddenly I was greeted in the streets by complete strangers shaking my hand. I loved it!

I did keep asking if anyone knew George, and they had all seen him at some point in the town but no one knew him well enough to make the introductions for me. Near the little port where all the ferries came in was a huge hotel with a vast balcony full of tables covered in perfect white linen. It was obviously the place to be in the town, and almost every day as we passed there was a wedding going on with beautiful people filling the terrace with music and laughter. Apparently it is the hotel where all the cast of *Ocean's Eleven* stayed, and it was on that very terrace that George copped his first eyeful of Lake Como and thought 'This is for me'. And who can blame him?

Sue Latimer and her husband Edward flew out the night before my birthday on 31 May to join us in celebrating. It was also our wedding anniversary, as I keep mentioning. The reason I keep mentioning it, dear reader, is because it is a bit of a sticky point between Michael and myself. When we got married we decided my birthday was a good date to settle on, as that way I would never forget my wedding anniversary. The problem was that after sixty years of waking up thinking it's my birthday it is hard to re-programme the brain to include a wedding anniversary too. Michael takes all these occasions very seriously and was appalled when we woke up in Venice one year and he presented me with two cards, one for each occasion, and I gave him nothing at all! I forgot, and I know I am selfish and awful but I did just forget. I have learned my lesson well, though, and now I am always ahead of the game. I carry the cards around with me as we approach the date just in case I get caught short! This time we had a great dinner for the celebrations and I had ordered a cake for Michael.

We made some lovely friends, Ken and Cindy, who hailed from Southern California and were wine buffs. Michael thought he had died and gone to heaven as they took him through the joys of Montepulciano! We started chatting one morning as we all sheltered from a shower or two. Coffee turned into lunch, which turned into dinner and we had a ball. The next day they invited us to join them for dinner in a local restaurant near the apartment they had rented. Ken also wanted us to do a bit of wine tasting.

When we arrived at the apartment there were six bottles lined up! He sat us down and presented us with a platter of delicious Italian salami and introduced us to truffle honey. He put a little smear on his salami and told us to follow suit. It was out of this world. What a taste sensation. The four of us then tasted the six bottles with no trouble at all. I cannot believe I sat there and sipped away with the rest of them. My poor digestive system went into overdrive!

Having decided that we were incredibly lucky to find ourselves in such a fruitful wine growing region, with so much to choose from, we descended to the restaurant. We sat in front of a window which ran the length of the restaurant. The view across the lake to the mountains the other side was breathtaking. As the sun went down we watched huge black rolling clouds spread out over the horizon like a velvet cloak. Lightning streaked down onto the water and the thunder followed, crashing like a rolling kettle drum in an orchestra. It was nature at her best, giving us a spectacle I would never forget. Meanwhile we ate superb pasta and Ken ordered a magnum of red wine. Yes, a magnum. It arrived with great ceremony at the table in a beautiful wooden box which was duly opened with great reverence and decanted into a fluted glass decanter. I looked across the table at Michael and raised an eyebrow. This was going to cost a fortune and we couldn't let Ken pay for it all! When the bill arrived Ken very firmly insisted on paying, and we left feeling very guilty but full of a warm glow of red wine. The next day we made enquiries and found another rather special eatery down by the lake near our hotel. This time it was Michael's turn to order the wine. He asked Ken about the magnum the previous night and confessed that we were feeling so guilty about all the expense.

'Not at all,' replied Ken. 'It is actually cheaper to buy a magnum if you think about it. We were bound to have at least two bottles of wine and as the wine I chose was 68 euros a bottle, two would have been 138 euros, and the magnum worked out at 125!'

Happy days!

We had another spectacular meal and rolled home to bed. Every moment of that week is etched in my mind. I could have sat on the terrace for the rest of my life. I'd love to think that maybe one day we could go back, if my fate could be so kind as to allow it.

9
TASTY TRAVELS

....

June 2012

After the thrill of Malaysia it was difficult to settle. It is always the same, isn't it? You come back from holiday and just want to go away again. Well, I was incredibly fortunate to be offered a series for ITV called *My Tasty Travels*. It involved driving round Britain in a sixties' camper van visiting wonderful holiday spots and learning about what we all get up to in our country towns. Each episode would finish with me taking on a cookery challenge. Like a typical actor I jumped at the chance, completely ignoring any warning voice in my head suggesting I might not be able to rise to the challenge. Me? Cooking? Pah, of course I was up for it.

It was agreed that Michael would be my driver and get me from A to B when I was not actually driving the van. Now, readers, the camper van was a piece of work. I had no idea how loved and cherished they are. Indeed, how expensive they are! We were in some market in Surrey and there was a board full of cards with camper vans for sale dating back to the early sixties and some of these vehicles were up for thousands of pounds. ITV had found me a lovely blue VW with all its bits in place, although the brakes left a lot to be desired. I found this out when we arrived in places like Devon and Cornwall and the director wanted me to perch on a cliff somewhere. I would haul on the handbrake and sit very still with my hand on the door handle ready to jump if necessary.

So many happy hours did we spend in the narrow lanes deep in the heart of the English countryside, with me driving at thirty miles an hour in front of a queue of very irate holidaymakers who were desperate to get past me. I was sworn at so many times. One day it was all too much and I responded to a driver who was tooting his horn at me endlessly with the finger. To my horror, as the car squeezed through, I realised it was a very jolly family of Mum and Dad, and two kids in the back, who were all waving at me and pointing at the van and giving me the thumbs up. I quickly waved back, furiously hoping my mistake had not been noticed.

The trouble is the world is divided between camper van lovers and those who just hate the whole idea. But for the duration of the series I was a member of this exclusive club and drove my van with pride. I nicknamed the van Batty, but kept forgetting whether it was male or female, so there is a great game to be had if you ever catch the series repeated on Gold or something, spotting how many times I change the sex of the camper van! It was such fun, though, and the directors would send me off on my own with a camera screwed to the window screen and a microphone up my jumper, and I would sail along these country lanes talking to my van and discussing all sorts of things as they came into my head. I had to try hard not to swear sometimes, and remember not to say anything rude about any of the team I was working with. Lots of different directors worked on the series and only one of them was insufferable, and I am afraid I did pass a few comments about him, but luckily for me the editor was on my side and spliced the offending comments out of the show.

The series began at Bovey Castle which was very grand. Start as you mean to go on, I say. However, sadly it did not quite live up to its very grand appearance. It was not entirely the fault of the hotel but the classic turn of the English weather. Although it was June, it was pouring with rain when we arrived and absolutely freezing. We were shown to our very beautiful room and did not really notice the chill too much, but by the time we got downstairs to have dinner it was creeping up on us. We were shown into a huge dining room which was incredibly grand, with gorgeous chandeliers and pristine white tablecloths and beautifully folded napkins. The trouble was it was empty but for one couple lost in a sea of white linen and crystal glass!

'Sit anywhere you like,' said the waiter smiling sadly. We made a beeline for a radiator that Michael had spotted in the corner, but as we sat down and put our hands out to warm them we realised it was turned off! We enquired of the waiter if it was possible to turn it on, and the inevitable response was negative, as the heating had been turned off for the summer. I have never eaten a three course dinner so fast in my life, and we did not bother with coffee. We arrived in our room to yet more arctic conditions. Michael rang down and asked for a heater which did arrive, thank God, and we snuggled into bed in T-shirts and jumpers. In the morning it took too long to heat up the room so I was desperately trying to decide what to wear for filming that day so I could get some clothes on. Doing my make-up and hair in a cold and drafty bathroom was no fun.

It was while filming this series that I first learned the difference between working on a drama and working for the documentary side of things. This was very much do it yourself, with a small crew consisting of cameraman, sound man, director and assistant, plus the producer who would pop in from time to time. I did my own make-up and hair and provided my own clothes, which proved quite a feat, as we did so many different episodes and the weather drove me mad! The hair was quite a problem as well, as it was always windy or raining and I did not possess hats. Thank goodness a couple of the coats I managed to acquire from Isme had hoods. In fact, I thought I instigated a bit of a coup all round in the wardrobe department by getting Isme to provide me with clothes. I got the benefit of personal shopping and they got the credit. I had a lovely time going to their offices and picking out my outfits. It was a good way of using my contract to the full. We aim to please!

One of my early challenges was to make a 'Chicken of the Woods' pâté. This involved foraging for the 'chicken' which was, in fact, a sort of fungi. I met these two lovely young men and they took me off to the woods. The fungi grow on the sides of trees in high banks running alongside the path through the very dense forest. I was very keen to do everything the right way and got very excited when I spotted some, clinging to a branch overhanging the bank. The only way to get to it was to walk round to the top of the bank into a field and then double back and find a hole in the hedge and climb through. I was so busy showing off and chatting to the camera I stepped into a rabbit hole and disappeared into the bush. Take two!

It took some stretching and sawing to get the stuff off but I did it and proudly carried my stash back to the camper van. One thing I learnt about, and absolutely love now, is that wild garlic can be picked so easily if you know where to look, and it is so delicious, much sweeter and more subtle than clove garlic. I made my pâté on a hot plate by the side of the camper van and managed to keep it out of the rain. I cannot tell you how many times in the next few weeks were spent running to and from the van with dishes trying to keep everything dry.

We then went to Petersfield Market and I had to persuade people to try my Chicken of the Woods pâté. Actually I did quite well, and thanks to a very pleasant elderly gentleman who had two portions I won my challenge.

Throughout the series I had one big problem: how to stop myself buying all the produce. Wherever we went I would get very over excited and buy ridiculous things that we would never eat in a million years. I still have cupboards jammed with chutneys and jams, and pickled vegetables. I must say that everywhere we went people were so warm and welcoming and so keen to show off their specialities.

One episode where I did experience a little hostility, or should I say overzealous competitive spirit, was when I went up against the WI. The challenge was for me to make a Victoria sponge to be served at a local school cricket match. To win, mine had to be judged as better than one produced by the ladies of the local WI. Now do not forget, dear readers, I had spent four years of my life playing Chris in *Calendar Girls*. This was territory I understood. The first day's filming I went for coffee with a group of the WI ladies, and the woman in whose house we were showed me how to make a rhubarb cake. We had a very jolly morning with coffee and cakes and then agreed to meet at the cricket match with our respective cakes.

Well, the crew and I pitched up in this field and set out the little Belling oven, which did not fill me with confidence. I started to make my sponge and guess what? It started to rain! The director Paul Vanesis was getting his knickers in a twist, rain always does this to a film crew. It is what one dreads more than anything. As I put the sponge into the Baby Belling he was already asking me when it would be ready.

'Well, it will take as long as it takes,' I snapped. 'About twenty minutes.'

'Well, we haven't got twenty minutes it must be nearly done.'

Sure enough, he lunged at the door fifteen minutes later and as we grappled, the door flew open briefly and my beautiful fluffy Victoria sponge was descending to the bottom of the tin as my sad, weedy voice called out, 'Nooooo!' and slammed it shut. But too late, disaster had struck, and my beautiful cake slumped to the bottom of the tin. The worst thing was that across the way the ladies of the WI were sitting in a car watching the entire proceedings with glee. In fact, Michael had arrived just before all this, and parked up only to be told, rather officiously, would he mind moving as he was blocking their view. I was in tears and furious with the director, who was not at all bothered.

'Don't panic. We have got a shop one on the side for disasters like this. No one will know the difference,' he announced airily.

'Oh yes they will,' I replied, pointing at the car of ladies waving at me. 'And anyway, I know it's a cheat and I won't do it. This programme should be real and truthful; I will do my best to make the cake look presentable.' I stomped off to get my raspberry jam which I had made with the help of a lovely lady in her shop the day before. I smeared the whole pot over a very thin layer of sponge and placed the other very thin layer of sponge on top and sprinkled it with icing sugar.

I was so upset and stayed away from my competition until the moment of truth.

Through all this drama the boys had all turned up and looked very smart in their cricket whites. Parents sat around picnic baskets drinking wine and chatting. It was a perfect summer's evening, except for me it was like a day at the coliseum. Gladiators, stand by your sponges. The WI and I walked towards each other and presented arms. Well, cakes. Theirs, of course, was huge: six inches of perfect sponge. However, if I remember correctly they had used plum jam which is not strictly correct for a Victoria sponge and, I learned afterwards, every one of them had made a cake and they had picked the best one! Six against one, it was hardly fair. While the boys finished their match, the cakes were cut up and labelled red and blue so no one would know which belonged to which party. Then the boys came to the table and each took a slice. I was keeping my ear to the ground listening to the comments. Whether

111

it was because they knew they were being filmed or not, I don't know, but they were so pompous about it all. They offered up comments like, 'Mmmm, I like the quality of the sponge on this' or 'Quality of the sponge is rather poor but I do like the texture of the jam'.

Needless to say, I lost and the ladies of the WI shook my hand with glee.

'Bad luck,' said one woman, hardly able to contain her delight.

Oh well, onwards and upwards. It reminded me of my school report: 'Lynda tries hard but could do better.'

One of the days that stick in my mind during the filming of *Tasty Travels* is the Watercress Line, when I got to drive a railway engine. I had no idea it would give me such a kick. This special line, which used to carry the watercress from the fields to the centre of London, is an obvious hit with the tourists. It is so beautifully cared for, right down to the period train station, waiting room and little café. I climbed up front and was blasted by the heat from the furnace. A very handsome young man was doing a great job of stoking the engine and another very handsome young man took me through the ropes. As we whizzed along the track I really felt the engine belonged to me. All these fanatics talk about the engines like their beloved mistresses. How they respond to the gentle, but firm touch, blah blah blah . . . but believe me when I hoisted the brake off and pulled on the throttle, it was like talking to a friend! I loved it. I swapped places with the stoker for the return journey and got very hot and bothered throwing the coal in. I cannot imagine what it must have been like for hours on end. But it left a lasting impression, and I intend to take my grandson, Sacha, if possible one day.

We went to Wales which was incredible. The sweep of Cardigan Bay and the ups and downs driving through the valleys was so impressive. It was like a film set. I am not a good sailor but managed to keep it all together when I was taken out by the local rowing club. I had to shout the instructions as we bounced over the waves. The Oxford and Cambridge Boat Race it was not!

They hold a huge seafood and fish fair on the quay in Aberaeron, and my challenge was to make a whole load of mackerel butties and chocolate brownies and sell them to make money for the rowers club. I did incredibly well and was down to my last three brownies. I told the director that maybe we should film me selling the last three as quite a crowd had gathered and it would make a nice ending. Instead she hauled me off to try every bit of fish on every stall in the market, which took forever, so by the time we went back to sell my last three brownies the crowd had gone home! There was a very nice lady with her daughter who offered to buy one, and Michael paid for the other two to get rid of them.

We moved on to Herefordshire and there was a wonderful event called the Mortimer Country Food Fair. My challenge here was to make a Welsh cake with a secret ingredient. So we spent a morning at a cider museum, where else? I met a lovely man who introduced me to the wonders of Perry cider. My head was spinning by the time I came out into the sunlight clutching a bottle of pear cider.

It was weird doing this series because I had given up the drink for several years. I've gone into a lot of detail in my first memoir *Lost and Found* about my somewhat difficult relationship with the drink: too much of it, basically. Then when I met Michael he too drank way too much, as it tends to go with the life in Spain. There is no doubt it had never done anything positive for me. Michael gave it up under doctor's orders – 'Stop drinking or you will have a heart attack or stroke in ten years!' he was told – and I bravely carried on for six months on my own but realised it would ruin my relationship with Michael. Although he did not exactly give me an ultimatum it was clear he was unhappy with having a girlfriend who would occasionally get legless. So I knocked it on the head and we had seven years of clarity.

Then one afternoon in Tenerife, in October 2012, sometime after *Tasty Travels* – we were having a little break before I started panto in Bradford – we were sitting in the sunshine by the pool, the way one does, and the couple on the next table had an ice bucket with a bottle of rosé in it chilling. The condensation was sparkling in the sun and it just looked so tempting.

'Do you think we will ever be able to have a glass or two of wine like normal people?' asked Michael wistfully.

'Well, let's suck and see,' was my response.

We ordered a bottle and slowly took our first few sips, half expecting to fall immediately into a drunken stupor. Oh no, not at all, it hardly touched the sides! It was so yummy. So we fell off the wagon and now drink like the rest of the silver sippers. However, I have a healthy respect for it and am still a little fearful of really getting hooked again, although I don't think that is going to happen now as I just don't have the capacity and it often makes me feel sick.

I do worry about Michael because I fear the wine bottle is becoming his solace. I don't want him to end up a lonely old man staring into the bottom of the glass. However, he needs something at the moment so I leave him be and then have a little nag every now and then and make sure he has two days a week clean. Nothing is easy, is it?

Regarding the pear cider, though, it had to be added to my Welsh cakes as this was to be my secret ingredient. The local hero, or heroine should I say, of Welsh cake making came to see me and seemed very friendly, but very confident her crown would not topple. I set up in a field next to the fair with the trusty hotplate and griddle. As usual as soon as I started cooking the rain came. After my disaster with the Victoria sponge I was really quite nervous, but God was kind that day, and I produced some real crackers. They were perfect. I carried them with care in a little basket covered with a red cloth across to the judges where my competition had already set her basket down covered with a blue cloth. The idea was the local band would do the tasting with the local celebrity, the wonderful John Challis from *Only Fools and Horses*.

It was such a lovely surprise to see him. We spent a happy hour going through old friends and then he was dragged off to perform country fair duties. He seemed to have the perfect life, I was rather envious. In fact all through the filming, as Michael and I saw more and more beautiful houses and picturesque settings, we talked about moving out of London and going back to Somerset, which is Michael's stomping ground.

I was also brought up in the country, and seeing all these wonderful villages and communities I was reminded of how life could be so much gentler and kinder than fighting one's way round London. There is so much talk these days about what is British and I think we are not proud enough of our culture. However, if you live in a city like London, or Paris, or New York, you can never really see the real culture because all these cities are global enterprises, full of every race and religion and culture from all over the world. All big cities are the same. Which is fine, but there is an attitude sometimes from city folk that somehow they are at the cutting edge, and all life experience is about them.

I say go back to your roots. Go back to the countryside and see what beauty there is. I think it would be wonderful if all children from inner city schools could spend a summer holiday on a farm. They could learn about the food they eat and where it comes from and they could learn too about life and death from the animals. Watch a lamb being born and then understand how to cook and eat it! I honestly think that if you showed some of these young people – the kids who get caught up in gangs and carry knives without understanding the damage they cause – a real slaughter, it would make them think twice. A knife into flesh for real is not like the telly or a PlayStation game. Life is cruel and animals can show children the good and the bad sides of their nature. Teach these children real respect for life, not the empty words they spout for effect in the streets. Show them fish in the sea and wild fruits and vegetables. That is our heritage and we should be so proud of it.

Enough of the sermon but I was so lucky to spend those weeks meeting people who strive every day to make a living from the land, people who love this country, and want to preserve it, in all its forms.

So back to the Welsh cakes, and blow me down my cakes are a huge success and myself and the Queen of the Welsh cake tied. What better result could there be? I hopped into Batty, my trusty camper van, and drove into the sunset to fight another day.

Things were not so jovial when we arrived in Cadgwith in Cornwall. This was an amazing community of fishermen. It is a tiny village literally on the edge of the sea. As we drove in, it is one way in and then straight out the other side. At the bottom of the winding hill sits the tiny cove with its array of fishing boats, each one with a tale to tell. There is a pub and a shop of all sorts and that is about it. Every window box, in every brightly painted house, is bursting with fresh flowers. It is magical. The idea was for me to go out and catch the fish of the day and enter in the competition that was held every other Friday night to raise money for fishermen and their families. The man who was taking me out was actually blind, and was incredibly knowledgeable about his work, and his life on the sea.

Unfortunately this episode was being directed by the one man who just should not be on the job. Not only did he think he was filming *Ryan's Daughter* with a cast of thousands, he was rude and insensitive and had no idea what he was dealing with in this very tight-knit community. To give you an example, as we drove in it was obvious there was nowhere to park. We had his car, the crew car and Batty, the camper van. A local man was just getting out of his car by the shop and our director ran towards him waving his arms and shouting, 'Excuse me! I say! We need your parking space, can you move your car? We are a film crew and we are filming here today so it is important we can park.'

The man paused only for a moment and then carried on past our ranting director into the shop. We were all cringing with embarrassment, and our lovely stage manager got hold of our man and dragged him back to his car and we all set off up to the top of the hill, where there was parking available. Word of this invasion quickly spread through the village and we got several rather unfortunate looks as we arrived on the beach for the fishing competition.

I tried hard to stay away from the director and went and met my lovely fisherman and his wife. Unfortunately I had my own huge problem to solve. I get seasick! I had discussed this with the producer and we agreed I would give it a try, but if things got too uncomfortable for me I could return to shore. Well, you can imagine how I was feeling as I climbed into this not over-large fishing vessel. I had had the pills, and was stern of heart, but as the clouds rolled in and the drizzle stung our faces and we bounced out to sea, I knew I was in trouble. Almost immediately my stomach started to heave. The director was having none of it and told me to make conversation with the fisherman while he filmed. I tried, oh how hard did I try, but every time I opened my mouth I was expecting a Technicolor rainbow! I was whimpering now and begged to be taken back. Finally the director relented, and I was unceremoniously dumped on the beach having had to walk the last few feet in the water to dry land.

I never really recovered for the rest of the night, which proved to be a nightmare, as our director went on to upset everyone. The catch of the day is weighed to great interest from the crowd, who were by now well-oiled and ready for their dinner which is cooked by all the women. People obviously pay as it is a charity event. Well, suddenly a man behind me says very loudly, 'I hope you people are paying for all this. When the BBC came here they paid us handsomely.'

'Oh, come on now,' replied Mr Diplomatic, our director, 'We haven't got any money, mate. Be grateful for the publicity.'

'We don't want the publicity,' chimed in another voice. 'We certainly don't want to encourage berks like you to come and soil our beach.'

I turned to Michael and whispered, 'How much money have you got on you?'

'Sixty quid,' he replied.

'Well, let's go and give it to the couple in charge and get out of here.'

Which we did, but as we were trying to leave without any fuss Herr Director rushed over and announced he needed me to do a piece to camera to finish the scene.

'I really don't think it's a good idea. People are getting quite hostile,' I said. But too late, the camera was rolling and there I was, standing in the dark with a bright camera light in my eyes, while behind me I could feel the group shoving and hustling, and making rude comments. I did my best to rush through it and then Michael and I literally took hold of each other's hands, and ran up the hill towards the car, leaving Mr Director to talk his way out. It was a nightmare. I felt so embarrassed by the whole episode, and I apologise if anyone from Cadgwith reads this – highly unlikely though it is – once they see my name!

Most of the series, though, came and went without any grief and I really did spread my wings and learn so much. From boat building in Lyme Regis to carriage racing in Wales. From Cornish pasties to high tea at Burton Court, an incredible house. The Cornish pasty episode ended in a most bizarre way. We met up with a lovely man, who had, arguably, the oldest Cornish pasty bakery in Falmouth. We made a huge giant pasty to take to the opening of the Falmouth carnival. When we arrived at the pub, celebrations had obviously been going on all day and the packed pub was up for a good time. It was quite daunting presenting my huge pasty to a discerning crowd. Well, I presume they must have been quite discerning as most of them came from the area and had probably been weaned on a pasty. After the judgement which seemed to go my way I was asked by the landlord if I would lead the pub in the carnival.

'I would be honoured,' I replied, envisioning myself aboard a fabulous float with a crown and long dress. An ageing carnival queen, but then again, I had just played the Fairy Godmother in the Birmingham panto, so I was well versed in waving! Oh, dear me, how deluded can one be. Health and safety had banned floats because one year there had been a tragic accident, where a child had fallen off a float and been run over and killed. This must have been devastating for the parents, I understand, but it was an accident and there had not been an endless series of similar incidents. Does it all have to stop because of one accident?

Anyway the good folk of Falmouth refused to lose their wonderful carnival so instead they do the whole thing on foot, starting from this pub. When we adjourned outside to join the festivities I was presented with a view of a field covered with hundreds of bodies all dressed in fancy dress. I, too, was dressed with the rest of the pub ready for action. But forget pretty dresses or crowns, I was dressed as a moose. And on my moose's head someone had kindly pinned a large badge on which was written in huge letters, 'OXO'. Oh the humiliation and yet more free advertising for Oxo, not something I encourage as they had dropped me from their campaign in 1999.

Anyway off we trooped and I walked with the group for about half a mile and then quietly veered off to the left and back home to London. Well, I had been up since five that morning and no one would really know it was me as I was covered with a moose head. It was great fun, though, and just lovely to see families all together out and enjoying themselves on a hot summer's night.

Talking of tea, I even got to create my own brand on a visit to the Tregothnan Estate. I added some manuka leaves (like the honey) – it was delicious, though I say so myself. It was extraordinary to drive around this beautiful wooded estate and suddenly come upon a hillside with tea plants growing and feel as though one had arrived, suddenly, in Ceylon. I made gin in Plymouth, and gave a 1930s dinner party on a train. I must say here that I learned to make a cabinet pudding, as it was very much of the thirties era, and it was delicious. I recommend you take a look in your mother's Elizabeth David cookery books and have a go.

We also visited some incredible gardens and the one that has stuck in my mind is Barrow farm. Mary Benger, the owner had spent fifty years creating this beautiful garden. Around every corner you were assailed by yet another scene of green and lush shrubs and huge trees standing guard across a perfect lawn. In another corner there was a bench to sit and reflect, and running water from a secret stream leading to a pool surrounded by fragrant wild flowers. It was the most extraordinary accomplishment and so full of vision. I even got to plant a shrub with her that she had recently been presented with as a prize. That is the one thing that struck me most about all the gardens like Painshill Park, and Dillington House, someone had the vision to plant these gardens for future generations to enjoy. They would never see the end product themselves except in their mind's eye.

I have so many memories from this time and writing about them has made me feel a little melancholy. I suppose I know I am so much luckier than many people, to have had the opportunity to see so many different sides of life, so I can look back fondly.

I just want to share one last adventure with you. We were down in Devon and visited Cockington Court, yet another beautiful establishment with exotic gardens. They have turned the stables and outhouses into studios for private businesses, like jewellery making, and wrought ironwork.

We went round and looked at all the different trades with an old friend of mine, John Labanowski, and his Mrs,

Brigit. He played my husband in *Calendar Girls* for the four years we were on tour. It was great to see them again and we had lunch in the restaurant there and shared happy memories in the sunshine. It was just lovely to see all these master craftsmen and women working away.

I was immediately drawn to the rocking horse man. Oh my goodness all my dreams came true at once. I know it must seem ridiculous, but all I ever wanted as a child was a rocking horse. I had this old tin thing which I made do with and, of course, on my tenth birthday I was incredibly lucky to be given the real thing. My pony Tiddlywinks! I have talked about her very often and very fondly. She dominated my life from ten to thirteen, until I tragically developed hay fever meaning that I could not go near her without breaking out in hives or peering at her through eyes partially closed and swollen. However, I never lost my desire for a rocking horse, and seeing the perfect specimens on display in the studio at Cockington Court just made me more determined. I announced on camera that all I ever wanted was a rocking horse, and pulled Michael into shot and shamelessly begged him to buy one.

'Look on it as an investment,' I announced. 'It is going to be an antique one day and our grandchildren and their children will cherish it forever.' I was being honest. These creations are quite something, and what the maker had done with these particular horses was build in a time capsule, so a child could put treasures inside their horse, and keep them secret for years. Oh how I wanted one!

Anyway, cut to Christmas Day and Michael presented me with a small box. I opened it and discovered a minia-ture version of the Cockington rocking horse. It was perfect in every way and I was thrilled with it. Michael looked at me very strangely and then burst out laughing: 'You silly cow! Do you really think I would give you that as your Christmas present?'

'Well, yes,' I replied. 'I love it, and we agreed we would not spend loads of money this year.'

'Well that's too bad because the real thing will be being delivered very soon.'

He gave me a big hug. I am a very lucky girl, I know. Well, lucky in love let's say and not so great in the health department, as we all now know.

The horse did indeed arrive, and Jack and his wife, Alison, put it all together in my window. It really is a work of art and better than any antique because we can use it. My grandson loves it, as do my sons and my hubbie, and it is so sturdy an adult can sit and have a rock! I often sit and rock looking out of the window and having a think about things.

It is a wonderful reminder of those weeks spent hurtling around the countryside in Batty my camper van, being paid to enjoy and learn and eat new things and meet lots of wonderful people.

Everyone should do it. Get out there and go on your own tasty travels. Life is too short.

10
HALFWAY THERE

....

October 2013

I couldn't believe it when October had already rolled around and I was over halfway through my twelve sessions of chemotherapy. Things seemed to have thankfully settled down in the stomach cramps area and I was finding that I was able to keep the pooh in hand. Well, not in my hand literally, you understand! So life, or my life as it had now become, was ticking along and I had become used to the rhythm of it all.

It is still amazing to me that days go by and I fill them with activity. A typical day in the life goes something like this:

I get up at 6.30 a.m. and I still make a hot drink for me and my hubbie with squeezed fresh lemon. I have a teaspoon of manuka honey in mine because it gives it a bit of sweetness, and manuka is supposed to have all sorts of healing powers. I then have to take ten different pills! I make a juice for Michael which is currently two handfuls of spinach, three sticks of celery, three small courgettes and a fresh pear or apple with the juice of half a lemon or lime and some fresh ginger. I pop everything into the smoothie maker for twenty seconds with some mango, Bob's your uncle!

The other one he likes is half a lemon, four whole oranges peeled and a little piece of fresh ginger. It is delicious and it provides you with all of your vitamins for the day. Michael has a glass of energised greens bought from Deborah Morgan's website too. I eat a bowl of porridge or natural yoghurt, again with a bit of honey. I have tried the gluten-free bread and it is disgusting, so I am going back to my toast and butter. There is no doubt I am developing a sweet tooth but I am careful to limit the intake.

We then go for a walk round the park. I leave Michael after three laps and he steams off, and I go back and clear up, put washing in and work out what I am going to give the hoard for dinner. I must say it is quite challenging coming up with different meals every night. I make a homemade tomato sauce every week and that lasts, in the fridge, for when the boys come in late and just want a pasta dish. I make myself shepherd's pie but often find it has been snaffled away in the middle of the night. And of course the hard one to cook for is Michael, as he does like his meat or fish and vegetables. I keep telling him it is an expensive way to live but he takes no notice.

Mind you he rarely eats lunch, so that helps, because then having finished my morning chores I retire to my bedroom and start up my computer. I do all the work emails first, and considering I am not really working as such there is still a good deal to cope with: answering requests for charity appearances and endorsements and things. I had a very unexpected request to write the fore-word for the 2014 *Giles* cartoon book. I was very flat-tered, and reading the cartoons brought back so many memories of my childhood on the farm. It was also a useful reference as to the history of the years gone by, and what went on. It seemed to me things just go round in circles in politics. I don't know if that is a good or bad thing.

I finish my correspondence and then open up my novel.

When I am writing I try to work for three or four hours on the trot, but since I have been having chemo I find that at about noon I just fall asleep at my desk! That is the signal to take more pills and lie down for a couple of hours. Then I get up and watch *Come Dine with Me* to which I am now addicted. I cannot believe people will make such idiots of themselves on TV. So many of the contestants are deluded about their cooking skills and some of the guests are just so rude. I love it!

By 6 p.m. I am always prepping dinner for whoever may be around. Sometimes meals in our house are eaten in shifts and my husband gets very cross because the lads all come in at different times, but I have become quite adept. The meals and dishes are all cleared away by 7.30 p.m. for *Coronation Street*. Helen Worth and Sue Johnston are good friends of mine and I never stop to marvel at how they manage to keep their performances so fresh. Actually most of the cast are wonderful and I like the humour. We did watch Hayley and Roy's story, and how they had to deal with her pancreatic cancer, with some fear and trepi-dation, and I must say I did shed a few tears. We both did, but it also got us discussing all the various issues surround-ing a terminal illness. The trouble with watching a story like that three times a week is that a discussion is unavoidable.

I have no idea whether it helps Michael to talk about the state of play or not. I sometimes think we have to talk about it as it is now a part of our relationship. We can't have deep meaningful, life-affirming sex anymore. Well we could try but my condition and everything that goes with it is a bit of a turn-off and cystitis rears its ugly head. I am being really honest and brutal here and I guess Michael might hate me for saying all this, but it has to be faced. I miss our physical life so much and sometimes there are no words and you just have to hold each other. Everyone going through an illness or crisis will understand where I am coming from, and if you haven't but you are about to begin this journey, I think you should know just how painful it can be. Sticking it to the back of your mind every day is not right. Being aware of your body, as I said before, is really important. It can tell you when it is the right time to cry or scream or just hold each other in an all-embracing silence.

I have tried very hard not to cry in front of the boys, and I am also aware that Michael is trying to stay positive as well, but every now and then things just well up and it is important to acknowledge these down moments. There was one night when after I had gone to bed I could hear Michael on the phone talking to our vicar, Peter Delaney, who had married us. Michael was literally sobbing his heart out. I felt so bad for him. When he came to bed we both just held each other and cried together.

'It is so fucking unfair!' was the *cri de cœur*.

'I know, I know, but there is nothing we can do about it except live our lives to the full for the time we have,' would always be my reply.

As I've said, I don't have a bucket list. One often hears about people in our position going off round the world. But Michael has a huge development to build, and why would I spend any spare money that we are certainly going to need in the future enjoying myself halfway across the world? Well, for starters the professor wouldn't let me do long haul, and secondly I could not deal with the guilt!

So our life goes on as normal, except it is in no way normal. On a bad day the cancer hangs over me like a black cloud. Sometimes I have such bad dreams when I have my afternoon nap that I want to hide under the duvet and never come out again. Those days are especially hard but that is when I drag myself to the kitchen and cook.

Towards the end of the month I noticed my tummy was distending again, so after my chemo session on Friday 25 October Justin Stebbing admitted me to the clinic for a scan. I always feel like such a drama queen when he does this. I don't want to be a bother and I worry about wasting money. However, it is not in my hands. Poor Michael must be so bored sitting in that very clinical room hour after hour. Sometimes, though, I think it might just do him good to sit quietly after a heavy week on site.

By Saturday I was ready to go home. Justin visited me at seven in the morning. That man really is a saint. When on earth does he manage to see his family? He told me I must starve my windy tummy by eating just yoghurt and white fish. Oh how dull is this? But I did as I was told for the rest of the weekend and blow me down by Sunday night I had no cramps, and no bloating and, best of all, I did not need to take any painkillers. I went to bed at nine and slept like a baby.

That lasted until 5 November when I was back in hospital again for the night, and there was not a sparkler in sight!

11
A REAL-LIFE PRINCE

....

November 2013

While I was juggling my pills and troubles, things went on in my life as a kind of backdrop, whereas before I would normally be chasing everything like a wild dervish. My first novel *Tell Me Tomorrow* had been published at the end of August, and had gone to number twelve in the top one hundred which was very exciting. I did not do as much publicity as I would have liked because most of the journalists only wanted to talk about the cancer, and at that point in my life I didn't feel ready to talk about it. I needed to understand what was happening to me before I could share any feelings about it all.

It is very difficult to talk about something when everybody who goes through it has such a different experience. I never talked to my sister Barbara about her lung cancer because I was too preoccupied in trying to make her feel better. I am the kind of person who copes with problems by trying to solve them. Is that an obvious thing to say? I don't think so, because I know people who would acknowledge that if there is a problem in their lives they either ignore it or absorb it somehow into their everyday life. However, at this point in my life I had no answers at all, so I preferred to hide away for a bit.

However, I had been almost forced out into the open because of the situation with the play. The production having to be cancelled had meant the potential audience needed and deserved an explanation. I also owed my fiction publishers, Simon & Schuster, some promotion for the novel. So I agreed to go on *This Morning* but I was determined to set my own agenda and get past the whole cancer thing quickly so the last thing people would remember from the interview, hopefully, was the title of my book.

Poor Phillip Schofield and Holly Willoughby hardly got a word in edgeways as I prattled on. But it worked and the studio went very quiet when I talked about my illness and explained that my white hair had been for my play, not a side effect of the chemo as the press had been quick to assume. When the interview finished Phillip whispered in my ear 'Well done, girl, it is good to see a pro at work!' But the papers only picked up on the hair and there was hardly a mention of the book – it was so frustrating. I would love to have gone round the country doing book signings, like I used to do when I was on tour with *Calendar Girls*, but I was just not well enough, so my appearance on *This Morning* was even more important to me. Because it was all so sudden I was still in denial, and did not fully understand what this was going to mean to me and the family and my career. It had just ended, like a kick to the head. Everything I loved and had ever worked for in my life was over!

I left ITV Studios, but not before I had stuck my head round the door of the make-up room for *Loose Women* and said 'Hi' to Linda and Donna, the ladies who make us look gorgeous. I was on automatic pilot, doing what I would have done in normal circumstances after a TV appearance. I seem to remember though that I was aware that my hands and legs were shaking and I felt light-headed. Then I went to meet Suzanne Baboneau, my editor at Simon & Schuster, Gordon Wise, my literary agent, and Sue Latimer, my theatrical agent. We were going to cele-brate the publication of my book. It felt just like the old days, sitting in Sheekey's drinking champagne. But again I think I was in complete denial. It was never going to be like the old days again. Ever.

I bumped into Michael Codron, one of the West End's most important producers. I worked for him on several occasions – in *The Sisters Rosensweig* at the Old Vic and *Noises Off* at the Savoy and *Look No Hans!* starring Sir David Jason – so there was much water under the bridge between us. I used to be in awe of Mr Codron, but now I had other things on my mind I greeted him like a long lost uncle, and arranged to have lunch with him soon. It is so weird that one is so conditioned as an actor never to miss an opportunity to engage with a potential source of work even if, as in my case, I was in no position to do so. Actually, in some ways, not being able to work made life easier. And being able to arrange lunches made me feel I was still part of the action. I was determined not to be forgotten!

I had recently met a fantastic lady called Judy Counihan. We had really hit it off when I went to see her for a general chat about work. We talked for ages, and I was pitching her an idea that my friend Catharine and I had had floating around for years, about domestic violence. Since there had been such success on the television lately with programmes like *Borgen*, *Wallander* and *Spiral*, a French series, Judy really wanted to try and do the same with a British cast led by me, which was such an inspiring idea and so encouraging as far as I was concerned.

It was great to have met someone who could appreciate my talents beyond Oxo gravy or being a Loose Woman, as I had really struggled over the past couple of years to persuade anyone in TV to give me a break. The answer was always the same, 'It's difficult to get away from that image and be taken seriously.' I struggled to understand why that was the case, because I felt that if I was popular with audiences – and the figures showed I was – why would an audience not also watch me in a drama? I did it in *The Bill* when I played Irene Radford after all. I found it especially frustrating when it seemed that when one format or idea for a television show works, then channels would stick with it until it was well and truly done then move on to the next hit. It often feels like channels just repeat the same old, same old, and mostly for the same old money!

I'd thought, now, maybe, I had the opportunity to collaborate on a new project involving my talent. I don't wish to seem big-headed but at the same time I was still not sure the powers that be had ever really recognised my abilities as a straight actress and it had been on my 'to do list' for some time. I wanted to make them sit up and listen to me!

I sometimes wonder, looking back over the last forty-five years, if there was more I could have done to get those parts I craved. It is a very touchy subject among actors, male and female, the question of the 'casting couch'. I do know people who have no compunction about sleeping with a director or producer to get the job, but it is not as easy as it seems! It takes time, months even, of chatting up the right person and then making a move and insinuating yourself into their lives. Frankly I couldn't be bothered and assumed talent will always out. But that is so naive and untrue! Luck is what everyone needs. Right time, right place and the right face.

I had been told at drama school I would never work until I was forty. I was not pretty enough for the juvenile lead and not ugly enough to play 'the friend'. It sounds very crude and cruel but if an actor does not learn very quickly his or her USP then all is lost.

I know my son, Michael, struggles with the same problem and it is even harder these days to be unique and different. 'Branding' is the buzz word. Nowhere in that idea do I see talent mentioned. I had always believed that one day I would find my role. The one part that would pitch me into the big time. It is an actor's sad lot in life to carry on, possibly never finding that moment, but always waiting and hoping that one day they will be discovered.

Now, here was I, basically being told by the big director in the sky that I might never work again. The moment could never happen. Now that is what I call a tough break.

I did not want to end my career as yet another blast from the past opening fetes and doing 'good works', but, having said that, one of my greatest pleasures as a result of being a famous face was all the charity work I had been doing over the last thirty years. It had taught me so many interesting and important things about life and introduced me to so many lovely people, both famous and not so famous. I had recently joined PRIME, The Prince's Initiative for Mature Enterprise, and I had been invited to a showcase event at St James's Palace.

This charity sits at the other end of the spectrum to the Prince's Trust which benefits young people. In contrast, PRIME is for people over fifty. The logo at the time said 'Age has No Limits' and I was first introduced to it a couple of years previously. The charity works with people over the age of fifty to help them turn their ideas, energy and experience into successful businesses. The work that they do is fascinating, and the invitation was to meet and greet and to enjoy the fruits of people's labours so far, all in the presence of Prince Charles. There was a huge array of very different ideas and products for sale. I met this incredible woman there called Alison Cork who has an online soft furnishings and home design business. We struck up an immediate friendship and decided we would go out to lunch and, over a few glasses of champagne, decide how we could find a way to make PRIME a bit more sexy! While we were talking a very jolly man called Mohammed came over and introduced himself and explained that he and his wife were fans of mine, which was nice to hear. He was worried that he would not get to meet the Prince so he had decided to stick with me as I was a better bet! So for the next ten minutes I was shadowed by this gentleman and sure enough, as I was asked to form a line so the Prince could say hello, there was Mohammed at my elbow. The court official gave me a bit of a look but

I just smiled sweetly. We had earlier been told that His Royal Highness did like to chat with people, but obviously time was of the essence, so would we please refrain from going into any stories about our latest family holiday, etc.! As the Prince moved in to shake my hand Mohammed eased in front of me and took over, saying: 'Oh how lovely to meet you, sir. I am with her you know,' pointing at me.

Well, he would not shut up and I could see the Prince was left in a very awkward position, so I put my hand on Mohammed's arm halfway through his long involved account of how he had started his business, and literally dragged him off, turning back to Prince Charles, saying, 'Thank you for your time, Sir, you must be very busy!'

He smiled and mouthed a thank you.

My friend Mohammed hardly seemed to notice and was off into the crowd to tell others of his good fortune.

At the beginning of September there was sad news as news broke that David Frost had died very suddenly of a heart attack. I was so sad for his wife and family. He was an extraordinarily talented man, and I had the pleasure of spending some time with him in New York when my friend Libby Reeves Purdie was his PA. I went to stay with Libby when she first moved to New York to work with Sir David, and that first time we went to see Bruce Forsyth on Broadway with Sammy Davis Jr. We had a great night and ended up in Régine's nightclub, which was the height of chic in the late seventies, let me tell you. We danced down Fifth Avenue at four in the morning with no shoes on. Happy days!

* * *

I was getting out and about quite a bit but every now and then I would be acutely aware that I was not the same Lynda physically. There was certainly no dancing barefoot anymore but even so I was disappointed sometimes when I couldn't even get through the day without falling asleep. I tried to stick to lunchtime events as that seemed bearable. But visits to the theatre proved a tad more difficult which depressed me, because I had rediscovered the Hampstead Theatre which was directly opposite my old drama school, the Central School of Speech and Drama at Swiss Cottage. I went to the opening of a new play, *Hysteria*, there.

I had many happy memories of this theatre, not just from the sixties, when it was more like a shack than a theatre, but as recently as 2005 when I had opened in a play there called *Losing Louis*, written by Simon Mendes da Costa, produced by Michael Codron and directed by Robin Lefèvre. In fact those three months from November 2004 until February 2005 were incredibly important to me in so many ways. I had met Michael in Spain in November and he started to come over at the weekends to visit me. I wanted to keep it all away from the press as my ex-husband was being very difficult and making things awkward for the boys and me, so I wanted to be sure that my relationship with Michael was solid before I introduced him to my sons. After all it had only been me and them for the last eight years! Alison Steadman was the other actress in the play and she devised the nickname Mr Spain for Michael. That was the secret password.

'Is Mr Spain coming over this weekend?'

He would arrive with his hand luggage full of Rioja and stay until Sunday night. In the week between Christmas and New Year I fell down some stairs and was on my back for three days (and not in a romantic sense!). Rehearsals were held up and I felt so guilty.

This play was such a big deal for me because it was a long time since I had been offered a decent role and I was so thrilled that Robin the director had thought of me. However, as is so often the case in my life, the reasons behind me getting the role were probably not as I would have wanted. There was a comedy element to the role and it involved a bare bottom! So it was nothing to do with my hidden depths as an actress then? But having said that it was a wonderful scene, and though I say so myself I pulled it off with aplomb.

I was playing the part of a neglected wife and in order to spice up my husband's sex life I agree to have my vagina pierced. He arrives in the bedroom and I turn with my back to the audience and seemingly open my dressing gown and show him the finished product. Under the dressing gown I am wearing a basque and stockings and suspenders with my bottom very naked. Why? The question begged to be asked, because for my own modesty I could at least have worn a pair of M&S knickers under the dressing gown and felt a little less vulnerable to my fellow actor, the fragrant Brian Protheroe. Why? Because the scene that followed would have suffered as I was asked to rush into the ensuite bathroom, with glass door, to make love to my husband who was suitably impressed by the piercing to ravish me against the bathroom door and all the audience see is my bare bottom pressed up against the glass!

I have to say it was very funny, and got a round of applause every night, but it was hardly Lady Macbeth and the offers from the Royal Shakespeare Company did not come flooding in.

The great sadness that cast a shadow across this whole period was the death of my father in January, followed by the death of my mother four weeks later, and being in this play that was set at a funeral could not have been more poignant or sad. I went to both funerals during the day and then did a performance in the evening. I was a wreck. However, as often happens in life, the tragedy led to great happiness as Michael was so supportive and it sealed our love for each other. I remember holding him one night and sobbing for the loss of my parents but at the same time feeling the overwhelming desire to take him and make love to him with a life-affirming need.

So here I was again, eight years later, in the foyer bar of the Hampstead Theatre with lots of old friends, including Alison, who happened to be at the same opening night as us. I had such a lovely evening and could almost forget that this was no longer going to be my life until someone would enquire about my health and I would come crashing back to reality. That has been the hardest thing to deal with so far, I think. Gradually I am becoming the face at the window looking in on a life I once knew, and trying to keep the smile straight on that face as it disappears into the distance. So there was a sadness creeping into my everyday life but I was determined not to let it win, and pushed myself to go out and have lunch and be social.

* * *

Then, just as I seemed to have found a sense of calm and pretended normality, once again disaster struck and I was back in hospital. Nobody really seemed to know what was causing these bloody pains in my stomach but they had become unbearable and my prognosis had now changed dramatically. I would not be ending my chemotherapy in December as hoped. The tumour markers were up and it would seem the course of treatment I had been on was not doing the trick. But Justin Stebbing always has a B, and C and D as far as I can see. I was told that I would probably have a couple of weeks over Christmas chemo free, then I'd be back into the routine again. The time allotted to my survival has diminished somewhat, though no one was able to give us a definitive answer. I know it is impossible to do that really, but it helps in a bizarre way to make plans. However, one thing was for sure, it was made clear to me that I would have to have chemo for the rest of my life to keep the thing at bay.

So at the beginning of November all of my social visits were called off. I missed the Christmas shopping day at Clarence House, which is a wonderful event. You can buy all sorts of rather camp presents for people: wine glasses engraved with the Prince's crest and baubles and plants and chutney and wine. The previous year we were feeling very flush and bought a watercolour print of Highgrove House painted by Prince Charles. It is number fifty-seven of a limited edition of a hundred, so hopefully the boys will hang that somewhere suitable when I am gone! As well as the shopping at Clarence House, I also missed an incredible party thrown by Robert Lindsay for his ex-wife

Diana Weston. Her fiftieth I believe! It was going to be a blast but I was just not well enough to go.

I had also been starting to organise my own party for Christmas. Please don't laugh, but I absolutely adore Christmas and the preparations are almost more exciting than the day. I had missed the last two Christmases at home because I was doing pantomime, so I was determined to make this one perfect. The only problem was that my son Michael would be in Wolverhampton, with Joe Pasquale, playing Slimeball in *Sleeping Beauty*. Ah he is his mother's son, we always get the glamorous parts! Also my stepson Bradley would have commitments to his mum and family, so I had decided to have our big Christmas lunch on 30 November.

Now that I was feeling so unwell, Jean and I decided we would find a lovely pub for my family lunch and make things easier for me. We found a beautiful pub in Hampstead called the Old White Bear which had a private room so all the family could let off steam without annoying the regulars. I got Michael to bring the tree into the house from the garage and Jean and I had a lovely day decorating it, the idea being we would eat first at the pub and then come home and have pudding and open presents.

On 11 December, when I woke on the day that I was due to go in for my last scan after my first series of twelve chemos, I had some of the usual niggling pain. By the afternoon it had increased, and when we sat down in front of Justin to discuss my scan and the results of the chemotherapy so far, he looked up at me from the famous screen inside the desk top and said, 'Are you in pain now by any chance, Lynda?'

As usual I mumbled something about yes it did hurt a bit but it would pass and not to worry too much.

To my amazement, and Justin's I should imagine, Michael burst out, 'That is not true! Please, Justin, take her into hospital because I am telling you now if you don't we will be back later and all hell will break loose.'

'I am inclined to agree with you, Michael,' replied Justin. 'So, Miss B, you will go now this minute and I am contacting Richard Cohen because I think we may have to do something about this tumour, which seems to have been growing under our noses and is causing you all this discomfort.'

Before I could say a word I was in a wheelchair on my way to the London Clinic, yet again, and I was not a happy bunny. Suddenly I was so frightened. I knew I could do nothing but put myself in the hands of these incredible surgeons and oncologists who work so hard to keep the likes of you and me alive. But it also meant I was not in control anymore and that scared me.

12
ALL CHANGE AGAIN

....

December 2013

A good deal of what happened to me over the next few days I cannot remember, and it becomes Michael my husband's story in a way. He sat with me in my room and I tried hard to chat, but the pain was so bad by now that all I could do was to concentrate on getting through each minute. It was a bit like giving birth to an elephant. But where in childbirth, the contractions start slowly and come in waves, with a little relief between them, these pains just swept over me relentlessly. I lay there from about four o'clock until ten o'clock, and although nurses would come in and check my vitals, and we would try and explain about the pain, nothing happened. I just hung between waking and sleeping. I could not really focus on anything. Poor Michael told me later he thought I was going to die there and then. Finally he went in search of a ward sister, and finally they gave me painkillers which provided me with relief for a while. I persuaded Michael to go home and said I would see him the following day.

That night, and the following night, were horrific. The nights are always the worst as we know. Strangely enough it might have been better to have been out in a ward rather than my private room, because I just began to feel I had been abandoned. No one came for hours, and the silence was only sometimes broken when a patient pressed their call button and that usually happened just as I had managed to drop off to sleep. My mind was slow but still going round in circles. What was happening to me? The pain hovered on the edge of my consciousness continually threatening to return. I was terrified and I was the one who was good with pain!

Finally morning came and with it a little hope. Mr Richard Cohen came to visit and explained that they were going to try and put a stent in to relieve whatever was blocking my colon. Then Mr Imbert arrived to tell us what he was going to do. This was the surgeon who put my port in originally, only to have to put it in again, but we won't hold that against him.

It was another long day of pain and a fog of confusion. Why was this happening to me? Dear Michael sat with me but I just couldn't respond to him and I begged him to go home and be with Bradley and Robbie. I just wanted to grit my teeth and get through the night-time hours that stretched ahead, in that dim blue hospital light, waiting. Eventually it was Friday 13th and time to go down for my operation. Friday 13th? It beggars belief! They came to take me down to theatre around 5 p.m., and Michael came with me. There was a very festive air about the place, as all the staff on that floor were getting ready for their Christmas party that evening.

Michael waited in the waiting room for about an hour and then the doors opened and he saw me being wheeled out with the anaesthetist, who was shaking his head. 'It is no good we can't do anything. We need Mr Cohen, and if we don't operate within the hour she is going to be dead. I am so sorry.'

The plan from day one really as far as Mr Cohen was concerned had been to remove the tumour in my colon as soon as possible. However, Professor Stebbing had needed to get at the cancer and stop its inevitable spread, although unfortunately it had already spread to my lungs and my liver. This operation was to insert a valve that would open and close and allow food to pass through the blockage.

Michael asked where Mr Imbert was, and the nurse told him he was on the phone to Richard Cohen. Michael waited by the trolley sobbing, as the nurses worked around him. Just then Richard Cohen flew through the door calling for a release form. All the nurses produced forms from different places! Michael offered to sign it but Richard Cohen said it had to be me if possible. I just about managed it, maybe I realised it would be the most important autograph I would ever write! Then Richard turned to Michael and said, 'Do you need me to read the whole form out?'

Michael just said, 'No, because I know she will die if you don't operate.'

'Yes,' said Richard Cohen. 'We will be ready to operate in about half an hour.' And he moved off towards the operating theatre. For the next fifteen minutes, Michael told me, the nurses stood around watching me in silence, then a phone call came through and the porters arrived to wheel me down. Everyone watched us go, and the sister put her hand on Michael's shoulder and wished him good luck.

At 6.30 the porters were pushing me through the automatic doors. All Michael could see was a hive of activity the other side. As I disappeared, and the doors slowly closed, he was completely alone in the corridor. The silence was terrible and he just burst into tears. He could not remember what he had been told about where to go to wait for the operation to be over, but he managed to find his way back to main reception. Someone then got through to the operating theatre and Richard came on the line and told Michael to wait in the family room next door to the crucial care unit.

So he made his way up to the third floor and found the room chock-a-block with relatives. They made a space for him to sit down, but within two minutes he was up on his feet again, pacing the corridor outside. He spoke to several of our friends and they all offered to come and join him with support. Their kind offers were so lovely but Michael told me afterwards that he suddenly realised that even though you feel alone and need comfort, you also need to stay in the zone. I suppose I felt the same in some ways with the pain, there are no words or even thoughts just an instinct to stick with the moment and get through it. Finally at about ten o'clock the room had emptied and Michael was alone. A few minutes later the lift doors opened and out stepped Richard Cohen still in his scrubs. He joined Michael in the family room.

'Is she OK?' asked Michael.

'She is doing fine,' replied Richard Cohen. 'I have taken out a huge tumour and I could see all the secondaries in the liver. I have had to add an ileostomy which is like a colostomy bag but for different functions.'

Here we go! In the shit again! The tumour was knocking at the wall of the colon and, just in time, Mr Cohen arrived to remove the tumour as it was literally perforating my colon. It was also in an awkward place. In fact they all agreed that not only did I have colon or bowel cancer, I had the most difficult one. I never do things by half! I've never been entirely clear on all the details, one of the reasons I never ask the questions is because the answers can be even more long and involved . . .

'She will be up in the crucial care unit in about an hour. So don't you worry,' Richard Cohen told my husband.

Michael said he burst into tears again and gave the surgeon a big hug. He was just so relieved.

'How long do you think she has got?' asked my dear hubbie.

'Two probably, that is about the norm.'

'Is that days, or months, or what?' said Michael.

'No, years,' replied Richard.

'Oh right,' Michael nodded. 'Right I can live with that. Thank you so much, Richard.' And he gave the man another hug.

When Richard had left, Michael went into the family room and sat down. Once again relief flooded through him that I had made it through the operation, but this new prognosis had shortened my life somewhat as originally it was two to five years. The problem now was whether the chemo would keep it all at bay.

Suddenly, sat there alone in the family room that December evening, it occurred to Michael that he was starving. He hadn't eaten all day and now it was eleven o'clock at night. He looked around but there was nothing. No vending machine or drinks machine. However, there was a large Selfridges carrier bag on the seat opposite with what looked distinctly like a bar of Cadbury's chocolate sticking out of the top. He went and investigated. There were several empty sandwich wrappers, and obviously the owner had either decided they had had enough, or they would be back for the chocolate later. Taking a quick look round first, my naughty husband then scoffed the lot and stuffed the bag into the bin. So if anyone who mislaid a large bar of Cadbury's Dairy Milk on the night of Friday, 13 December 2013 happens to be reading this, please accept our humble apologies. We owe you one!

Finally, a nurse came out from the crucial care unit and told Michael she was going down to fetch me now and would be up in fifteen minutes. Sure enough the lift doors opened fifteen minutes later and I was wheeled out. Michael said he could hardly see me for all the tubes and wires going into me, but I was quite chatty and lucid.

'Give us thirty minutes to plug her in and sort her out and you can come in,' explained the nurse.

Michael came and sat with me for about three-quarters of an hour. I can remember him being there holding my hand, but it was dark in the ward and I was so hot and sweaty and disorientated I just clung on to him.

When he got up to go I called after him, 'Don't forget, Michael, there is lots of food in the freezer for you and the boys.'

'Typical!' thought Michael as he made his way home. 'Her answer to everything is to make sure we all eat.'

But he was smiling for the first time in forty-eight hours.

The next day Michael came to visit from eleven and stayed until about 1.30. The crucial care unit is not the best place to try and hold any sort of conversation, not that I could have done so anyway. I was in pain and still very drugged up, and the nurses were in and out all the time checking up on me. I wanted Michael to go home and rest.

The next twenty-four hours are a haze to me now. I just remember pain and noise of other patients crying out in the night. Sometimes the nurse, who was so brilliant, would come and just dab me with cool wet flannels or rub my back. I was so uncomfortable and kept trying to turn on my side to sleep, which was impossible. I had tubes up my nose which were driving me mad and my throat was so sore. It was just an endless stream of discomfort. Then I would have very clear lucid moments and I watched a family opposite me through the glass partition, sitting with a woman in the bed who was obviously very ill. I asked a nurse what the problem was, and she told me the woman had had a brain operation and was in a coma. That shut me up and I felt very lucky to be able to feel my pain.

Michael visited and I sent him home as usual! But on the Sunday, he told me later, as he was coming to visit, Justin Stebbing popped out of the lift and greeted him. They discussed the success of the operation and Justin apparently told Michael that he gives all his clients three lives.

'Lynda has just had her first one. Do you think you and Lynda would be up for putting her up for trial drugs any time soon?' he asked.

'Yes, we will do whatever it takes,' Michael answered.

'Good. So let's go and see how your wife is getting on.' As Justin turned one way Michael went the other, towards the crucial care unit.

'Where are you going?' asked Justin. As Michael pointed to crucial care, he added, 'No, she is back on the ward now, much nicer.'

They both entered the room together and each took hold of my hands. I looked from one to the other.

Michael told me afterwards that I looked like a rabbit in headlights.

It was a very apt description because I have never felt so frightened in my life. I thought they had both come to say goodbye!

I was sixty-five years old and had hardly ever been in hospital, let alone an operating theatre, and I certainly had not found myself lying in a bed attached to eight intravenous drips before! The word 'random' sprang to mind. How random is life? I have no control whatsoever, and I could only hope there was a plan to get me out of this mess.

13
HOLDING ON TO THE FESTIVE SPIRIT

....

Christmas 2013

So there I was in bed on the fourth floor of the London Clinic waking up in my corner room surrounded by tubes and a pain in my tummy. I had no idea how close I had come to death but was feeling very sorry for myself anyway. It was bad enough having to deal with cancer, but a major emergency operation was a step too far. Had Richard Cohen not arrived on the scene I think my insides would have covered the floor. I still had my colon which is the long tube that goes down through your body and my spleen which has something to do with the stomach. I am so ignorant of what went on and I apologise to anyone reading this for not giving you the detailed version of things. After all, it took me ages to work out that bowel cancer and colon cancer are the same thing!

While recovering from a major operation is sometimes torture, there are moments of humour too. That first day of consciousness in one's bed is a revelation. The nurses were all so jolly and matter of fact and made everything seem perfectly normal as they emptied a catheter while chatting about their night out. All day long the patient gets snippets of the real world outside while battling rubber sheets and mechanical beds. One minute I would be gazing out of the window at a perfect blue December sky, catching a breeze from the crack in the open window, and the next I was reeling in agony trying to sit up. The tube up my nose was making me retch all the time and I was constantly fiddling with the bloody thing. All my drips were explained to me and then I completely forgot what they all did within a minute.

I knew by now that I had a huge scar and when the nurse came to change the dressing I gazed down in amazement at what could only be described as a very long zip going from my chest to my pubes. It looked bizarre with metal clips all the way down. To the right of the zip was a pouch which I really could not fathom out. I had been informed that the bag hanging down my left side was taking away the bile from my stomach, and as soon as the stoma kicked in I would no longer have that particular attachment. Stoma? To my utmost horror I was then introduced to the attachment on my right side. A very pink strawberry was poking out of my stomach! This was a step too far for me. I may have a high pain threshold but I was about to discover I do not do body parts, however neat.

I shut out all thoughts of what I was supposed to do with that straight away. But Michael, as usual, came to my rescue. While Richard Cohen was examining his handiwork he asked Michael if he wanted to look. Michael could not refuse the challenge and came round to the side of the bed. I had my head turned away as I could not bear to look, but my dear husband listened attentively to everything Richard told him about how it would all work and then announced, 'Thanks, Richard, that is really interesting but isn't it amazing how it looks like a little willy!'

We all burst out laughing and somehow I managed to relax about the whole thing. As the days went on and I slowly grew more accustomed to my plight, we nicknamed the stoma 'Furby' because it started to make the most incredible noises like those Japanese children's toys. It sort of chirruped or whimpered depending on what was going on! The lady who wins the prize for hard sell of the stoma bag is Rebecca Slater, this truly inspirational stoma nurse, who took Michael and me through every aspect of the wonders of a stoma bag.

'You will never want to pooh normally again,' she announced. 'So many of my patients say they prefer to have a bag.' Well, the jury is still out on that as far as I am concerned, but at least Becky made me feel more secure about it all. However, it was a few days before I saw the wonder of the workings of a stoma. There were many more hoops to go through before that, I am sorry to say.

The first week was a dark tunnel. I managed to get through the days in a kind of bubble. The routine of hospital life kicked in. I would wake up and wait for my painkillers and try to drink some water to get rid of my parched throat.

I made a terrible mistake the second or third night by pulling the drip out of my nose. For a brief few blissful hours I was free of the thing, and the retching and trying to be sick. All these wonderful actions, of course, pull the stomach muscles and my muscles were being held together with metal clasps. Every time I coughed it was agony. So the fact I had stopped the retching by pulling out the tube was a job well done as far as I was concerned.

Then the nurse informed me I was not getting the benefit of the intravenous feeding so they were going to have to put in another tube. Now, folks, here's the thing. The first time they put the dreaded tube up my nose I was unconscious, but this time I was awake and absolutely terrified! It was like a bad dream and it still does return to haunt me. It is similar to the feeling when the doctor puts a spoon in the back of your mouth and you want to retch. But this also scratched the edges of my nasal passage and made my eyes water. How long does it take to push a tube down your nose into your stomach? Too long!

The whole coughing business of course is there for anyone who has been through an operation. And the Kathy Bates moment when the physiotherapist appears in the door! This moment came the second day for me, in the form of a very pleasant young man who seemed very malleable, if you know what I mean!

When this very pleasant young male physiotherapist came round, I whimpered, 'Oh no,' in my best Dame aux Camélias voice. 'I really don't think I am up to this at all. Can you come back next week?'

Not on your Nellie. That seemingly sweet young man was across the room before I had finished speaking and was levering me up out of bed!

Stuffing a pillow into my arms he said, 'Now make yourself take deep breaths and cough.'

Oh my goodness, the pain. How could he be so cruel? He was smiling all the time as I tried pathetically to produce a semblance of a throat clearance. Then suddenly he was gone and I was lying back in a pool of sweat gasping for breath like a fairground goldfish.

Ten minutes later the healthcare ladies came to change the bed and there was another fifteen minutes of acute pain trying to get me to the bathroom and set me down on a chair for a wash.

The first time I had warm water splashed over me I almost cried with joy. How amazing that something as simple as water can bring such relief. The lovely girl who washed me those first few days was a naturally gentle person. She would wash me so carefully and apply cream to my skin so expertly it was better than any five star spa I have experienced. My eternal gratitude goes out to these carers.

So then I was clean and dry. I was set down in a chair and told to try and sit up straight for fifteen minutes or so. I stared blankly at the TV screen on the wall. My mind had shut down, I think. I believe this is the only way to deal with these things: just let the routine carry you through, do as you are told and hang on in there.

I went back to bed and waited for more painkillers. I had this self-medicating button I was supposed to press every ten minutes or so, but quite honestly it was not doing anything except making me feel sick. Eventually I had a visit from Jamie who deals with all the patients' pain relief. We discussed the merits of the button and I tried to explain that my pain was localised and I thought it was in my stomach where the cancer was, not in my muscles or working parts. He changed the medication to something more like paracetamol which helped, but this did not go down well with the next ward doctor who came to visit. He flounced in and I think he thought he was in an episode of *Casualty*!

'Morning,' he threw across the bed at me. 'Who have we here, nurse?' He took the proffered notes with a flourish.

'I'm Lynda, and can I just say that I have worked out my meds with Jamie and things are going much better.'

'Well I don't understand, we have given you pain relief in your button, Miss Bellingham. You probably do not understand how we go about deciding these things, but I can assure you we are correct in our administration of pain relief.' He turned to go.

'Um, sorry, Doctor, but you are wrong,' I called after him. I think it must have been the drugs that made me so brave, because normally I am such a wimp about confrontation.

He stopped and tossed back his floppy hair.

'I am sorry?'

'Well I am sorry too. It is my pain, not yours, and maybe I might just know a bit more about what is going on and what works and what doesn't. Are you not taught to listen to your patients?'

Doctor Kildaire turned on his heel and left, leaving me and the nurse in fits of giggles. Well I would have been giggling if it didn't hurt so much!

I never had a visit from said doctor again, and the meds were left as they were, and it was all fine. The thing is, as time goes on and every day is spent not only navel gazing, literally, but having to work out how to feel better, the patient feels the problems better than any doctor can guess. I think that it should be a dialogue between the two.

The days seemed to pass quickly and Michael would always come in to visit in the afternoon with cards and letters of goodwill from friends and well-wishers. I asked him to tell people not to send flowers because it is such hard work for the nurses. Yes they are lovely to look at, but there are never any vases and when the water starts to smell and you can't empty the vases yourself, it is just a chore. I could hardly ring the bell for a poor hardworking nurse to sort out my flower arrangements. Priorities exist and saving lives tops flowers any day. I was certainly grateful that my life had been saved.

For the first few days I could not eat solids so there was no meal break to look forward to. I would watch the darkness descend outside and dread the onset of bedtime. Bedtime? That's a joke, the whole time was bedtime. But once again the wonderful nursing staff would come to my rescue. As I watched the minute hand move inexorably across the face of the clock on the wall in front of me, and toss and turn in my sweaty pit, suddenly Sister would appear with a cold bag and put it behind my back and just hold my hand, and chat about this and that. I am sure she had so many other things to do, but she gave me those few minutes to settle. Then I would sleep for a couple of hours then wake again, sliding off my rubber pillow. Oh my goodness it was awful.

In fact nobody could quite decide why I was so hot and sweaty. I eventually worked out that, in one week, I went through my entire menopause, because I had had no HRT for months, having come off the medication and suddenly all hell had broken loose in my body. There must have been enough raging hormones to jump start a car, I would have thought. I have had no symptoms since, and can only assume this was the case. Be grateful for small mercies, I say.

Bring on any change of life, it has to be better than death!

14
THE BEST-LAID PLANS GO TO WASTE

....

Christmas 2013

By the time all of this had happened, we were into the second week and Christmas was nearly with us. In between trying to walk upright with a walking frame and coughing without choking, I was obsessing about what Michael was going to do about Christmas dinner.

'Don't worry, I will do all the cooking,' he announced one day. This from a man who has trouble making a salad! I was devastated that all my planning was falling apart. My dear sister, Jean, knew only too well how much the whole shebang meant to me, and she had been helping me from the start to gather all my supplies together for Christmas. In fact we had been scheduled to go to the wonderful Christmas fair at Olympia together as we had done the year before. At the fair they sold everything imaginable you need for a perfect Christmas. I had ordered this amazing organic turkey due to arrive on 19 December. Did Jean think Michael would be able to manage?

Her silence spoke volumes. I could not even rely on Jean to help him prepare it as she is a veggie and would not touch the bird with a barge pole. So I had to write all the instructions out for Michael. Fortunately the turkey came with perfect instructions so that bit was sorted, but the timings of the extras proved a problem!

However, due to the fact that I had been planning Christmas since the end of October I had most of the gig under control. I was still cooking whenever I felt well enough, and had a list of dishes I was going to produce over the festive season. I know this must all sound completely nutty to many of you, but Christmas is such a joy to me, and I always want it to be perfect.

I had been collecting bits and pieces for the boys' stockings as well and I was keeping them in a box at the bottom of my bed. I know they are grown up now but they still love their stockings. I also had my step-grandchildren coming over Christmas, Cooper and Oakley, and my grandson Sacha. I decided not to go too mad with the decorations round the house, but just put out a few of the favourites, like the wreaths and table lights and garlands! At least I was not setting my Christmas table yet. Years ago I was filming in Prague and was not going to arrive home until Christmas Eve. So I decided to do all the table settings, and decorations and the tree, in my dining room before I left in November. I locked the door so the boys would not find out and set off. Sure enough I arrived home Christmas Eve and after a bit of a dust things looked lovely!

So from October, with every trip to the supermarket I would add to my Christmas cupboard, which was now bulging with mince pies, candied fruit, Twiglets and Turkish delight. I bought all the wine and spirits too – not that the spirits ever really got drunk as no one in our house drinks them, but I like to know they are there in case. My intention for Christmas Day was for everything to be on hand for everyone because it is the one day of the year when anything goes. So basically I was set and ready to go. Except I wasn't going anywhere. I was going to be in hospital.

I seem to be one of these people who think that if I have thought about something, arranged something, even dreamed of something, then it will happen. In many ways this is very positive and a good way to view life. However, reading back through some of my thoughts and diaries since being diagnosed with a terminal disease, I am beginning to realise it can be incredibly stupid! There are some things one just can't change. In this case it was Christmas lunch. Even in my darkest hour sliding around on my rubber sheets in a sweat in the middle of the night, it never occurred to me that I would not be at home on Christmas Day at the head of my table with my family around me. I had thought about the moment, lived it, organised it and dreamed it. Of course it would happen. But when it finally sank in this was not going to happen, I just burst into tears and when I wasn't crying believe me I spent a good deal of my time trying to keep those tears at bay.

The nurses were most solicitous. 'Don't cry, Lynda, come on, you have done so well. You are going to be fine.'

'I'm not crying about the bloody cancer,' I blubbed. 'I'm crying because I can't do my Christmas lunch. The cancer is something I can do nothing about but I was so sure that

I would be home for Christmas lunch that I am disappointed in myself. Sorry, girls, I appreciate your sympathy but I am heartbroken.'

What a silly cow I am really!

At least all of the Christmas preparations had taken my mind off the medical side of things, although I did seem to be making some progress. I finally came off my bags of fish and chips. This was the nickname given to the bags, big plastic ones full of liquid food, that arrived every twenty-four hours to be given intravenously.

Now I could order something to eat, but what? Everything tasted of nothing until I discovered the hospital kitchen's shepherd's pie. For some bizarre reason it tasted delicious and became my staple food, apart from yoghurt and honey or porridge for breakfast. Then it was Furby's turn to start to work. Oh what joy, listening to my bag fill up. Apologies if you are reading this anytime near a meal. But spare a thought for us poor folk with a Furby!

The young waiters who brought the food would make me smile (I could raise a smile but laughing was still a painful process, don't forget). They would breeze in and pull your bed table across and dump your food just out of reach, and then they were gone before you could ask them to just adjust the table closer. Every mealtime was spent trying to angle myself in such a way as to be able to pull my food closer to me. Or if that failed, to hold a spoon steady, while it made its precarious journey from the tray to my mouth. Surely someone could offer a quick lesson in the logistics of patient/food administration?

My walking was coming along slowly, although clinging to a walking frame is not very good for the spirit. I really did feel as though I had skipped ten years of my life and was now in my seventies. I had asked Michael to keep the boys away. They had all expressed a wish to come and visit, but I was not ready to see them. I knew that if they saw me now, not having seen me for a couple of weeks, I would look very frail to their eyes. I did not want the illness to get to them. It is one thing to deal with a situation that they could forget about from time to time, when I was able to go about life with some degree of normality, and quite another to be faced with the reality of facing a sick old lady hobbling down a corridor.

I was proved correct about this when one day after Christmas Robert came to visit. I was trying to get back to my bed before he arrived, as sitting up in bed I could pretend I was more sparkly than I actually felt, but as I was shuffling towards my room Robert came round the corner and literally bumped into me. The look of dismay and horror that crossed his face was heartbreaking. He recovered himself very quickly and took my arm, but I knew he was shocked. I guess I wanted to make sure that my sons would always retain an image of me, not as an actress – they had so many of those in photos and videos – but the one in their mind's eye that should automatically spring up when they think about 'mother'. Every mother wants to be perfect for their children, don't they? Of course so often we think of how old our parents are. It's like looking at photos of teachers from school. They seemed so much older than when one looks at them now from a distance, and most of them were only in their early twenties.

I have such clear memories of both my boys as young children looking at me very seriously. Taking in every line on my face. It felt like they were reaching for my very soul. I have thought about this illness that has taken me over and I can already see what it is doing to my skin and my muscle tone, and although I am no Sophia Loren I have a certain pride about myself. I was quite fit, and certainly when the boys were younger I prided myself on being able to keep up with them on all levels. Now I was beginning to feel vulnerable. Michael, my husband, was kind and generous enough to throw an imaginary veil over the body that was no longer the one he might remember from better days, but children are much less forgiving. It felt like the moment when they withdraw from you and lock the bathroom door, I now wanted to shut my door and hide my new/old body. I was invincible once, in their eyes, and I was determined to remain so to the end.

In between the usual everyday chores of life on the ward I would be hauled off for the odd X-ray or scan. Every manoeuvre was a major battle and sometimes I wanted to scream in frustration. Trying to get onto an X-ray table that was too high, with my tubes in the way and my scar pulling in agony; lying still while a nurse searched for yet another vein into which to plunge a needle. Please don't think me ungrateful, I am fully aware of how lucky I was to have all this care and attention, but there are times when it is all just too much to bear. I hardly thought about the end result either. OK I knew I had to recover from my operation and get back onto the chemotherapy, but all that business of having cancer seemed to belong to a different person!

There were days when I did feel as though I was making headway, and as Christmas Day approached I concentrated all my efforts on my arrangements. As far as the hospital and all the nurses were concerned, it would be business as usual, but I had got Jean to bring me copious supplies of chocolates and mince pies and nuts and tins of biscuits, and was handing these out to whoever came to visit. Of course the nurses would have a little party and the party hats were worn and we all managed to capture a little of the festive spirit. I had written an essay of instructions for Michael for his Christmas dinner and he was being very cavalier about the whole thing.

'You watch me,' he bragged. 'It will be a doddle!'

We arranged that the boys and my stepdaughter and her two boys, and my sister and my nieces, would all come and visit Christmas morning, before they went off to have lunch. I took extra care to brush my hair and put on a new nightie, and was sitting in my chair when they all arrived. They could hardly all fit in my room, but it was so good to see them all. Looking at the photos we took on the day, I look pretty grim to be honest, but they were all pleased to see me, bless their hearts. After they had all gone Michael stayed for a while longer and we had a little tear. I felt like a child being left out of the party. He was being so brave but I knew he was very near to tears all the time too. But I chivvied him up and sent him packing to do his worst. Or best.

I was alone. For the first time in my life I was not with my family in front of a big glittering Christmas tree surrounded by love and laughter. I had had two Christmases in the last two years where it had been just me and Michael, when I was in pantomime, but I had never been completely alone.

Would there be a Christmas for me next year, I wondered? I suddenly felt very vulnerable and aware that my life had changed irrevocably, and I was not too sure which way I was heading.

My thoughts were interrupted by my mobile phone ringing and my husband asking me about potatoes.

'How long do I boil them?' said the masterchef.

'Ten minutes or so and then drain them and give them a good shake and stick them in very hot oil. How long has the turkey been in now?' I added.

'Three-and-a-half hours and it is bloody done, so now I am all behind,' said a very flustered husband.

'Surely it can't be done yet,' I replied unhelpfully. 'Check again with the thermometer thingy they gave you.'

'I have done all that, so now please let me just get on. Speak to you later.' The phone went dead. I decided to ring Stacey, my stepdaughter, and check out the state of play.

'Everything is fine, don't worry, Lynda. Dad is just getting his knickers in a twist because everyone is starving and the timings are a bit off,' she laughed, and I could hear whoops and shouts in the background.

'Oh dear, well unfortunately there is nothing I can do to help, Stacey, but keep me posted.'

After several more increasingly panicked phone calls from hubbie, everything went quiet, and over the next hour I received several text messages with pictures of potatoes and sprouts and the turkey's bum and finally lots of happy faces. When Michael rang late in the afternoon I could tell he was as pissed as a cricket but I could hardly blame him. He had done it, even if the potatoes did take forever and they lost the Christmas pudding!

On Boxing Day I had a visit from Peter Delaney and his partner Paul de Ridder. Peter has not only been a dear and close friend for many years, but is also the man who married me to my previous husband and to Michael, and has christened my two sons. He suggested I might like to take communion with him. I am not a very good Christian and do not go to church often enough, but I enjoy the services immensely when I do go. I think this has a great deal to do with Peter's talent as a vicar and orator, as much as anything, but I was very touched by his offer and accepted. To my utter surprise I was in tears by the time he had finished, and so moved. Why I should have been so surprised I really do not know, but I was, and also ashamed that I could be so casual about my beliefs, because at that moment I gained such comfort from the simple service and prayers that Peter performed especially for me.

My faith has struggled considerably since, I am afraid to say, and many times I have tried to pray but given up in despair. It is almost impossible to understand why bad things happen to us, and especially when at this point in my life I was prepared to accept my lot as long as he looked after my husband and my boys. But who knows if the great man will oblige?

I always think that the days between Christmas and New Year are completely lost; something and nothing. A time to recover from the excesses of Christmas Day and regroup, I suppose, or to rush out and spend yet more money in the sales. For me they were more hours spent learning to change my Furby bag, oh joy, and walk upright. My scar was healing very nicely, and I was finally down to just one intravenous drip. I remember one morning staring down at my stomach and thinking how on earth I had got here, and so quickly it seemed. One minute I had been navel gazing in a bikini, aged twenty, pulling my stomach muscles in so I had that slightly concave stomach between my hip bones, and now I was faced with a mound of flesh covered in white train tracks and adorned with a plastic bag like a large Elastoplast. My legs were like two sticks poking out from my nightie and suddenly overnight I had flabby arms and liver spots on the backs of my hands.

I refused to linger on these awful reminders of my impending doom. I made a promise to myself that when I got out of hospital I would make sure I always dressed smartly and took care of what was left. Before Christmas I had discovered the wonderful world of the catalogue, something I had appeared in with Isme, naturally, but never really investigated. Oh, the magic of pointing at an object of desire and writing down the code then hearing the doorbell a week later and a nice man handing over a parcel. Fatal if you let it take you over, I know, but fabulous if you needed a boost of confidence, and I reckoned I deserved a bit of a boost now and then.

I had regular visits from the wonderboys Justin and Richard, and the discussion had begun as to how soon I could start the chemo again. The problem being that one of the drugs given to me as part of the chemo, called Avastin, thins the blood and makes the healing process very much slower. Naturally, Richard Cohen was very protective of his handiwork and wanted the wound to be completely healed. Finally it was agreed I was to be dismissed from hospital on New Year's Eve, in time for the celebrations, whatever they might be.

I was terrified of leaving. Can you believe it? I actually asked if I could stay a bit longer. 'This is quite a normal reaction,' the sister on duty told me. 'You will feel very lost and out of your comfort zone but believe me, it will only be for a short while, and you will soon be back in the swing of things.'

Well, like it or not, I was discharged. I pulled on some jeans and realised they would squash Furby so I left them undone and covered up with a big jumper, making a note to myself to work out new fashion accessories to accommodate my new appendage. I made my goodbyes to all the fantastic nurses and health workers and felt very tearful. I stepped out into the chilly winter morning and, like everyone else when they leave hospital after a long stay, I marvelled at how nothing had changed and the world was carrying on as usual. We drove home and I held a cushion over my tummy as we hit the road bumps. I could not wear my seat belt as it fell right across the new scar and Furby. Everything seemed strange and alien to me, including my own body.

Walking into my flat after three weeks away was like being the mole in *Wind in the Willows* when he is called by his home to return. It was such a comfort to feel and see all the familiar smells and sights and sounds. The Christmas tree was still there for me to enjoy, and my presents were all piled underneath waiting for me. I had a mountain of cards and I was just so touched by all the comments and good wishes. Now that I was home again, I didn't quite know what to do with myself, but I went and got into bed on Michael's instructions. What bliss it was to be in a proper bed with crisp white sheets and the smell of lavender. I lit some candles and revelled in the feeling of my head on a pillow that was not rubber. I looked round my bedroom at the photos and all the familiar nick-nacks that make up one's life, and I seemed to see it all through new eyes. I was so pleased to be alive. Alive but for how long? Actually at that moment it didn't really matter because each minute was a lifetime to me and yet each imagined lifetime only lasted a minute. It is so hard to explain about time throughout this whole process. It is a cliché to say I have savoured every moment, but I have and it was quite thrilling.

It was the eve of a new year and I could hardly begin to imagine what lay in store for us all. We opened a bottle of champagne and toasted each other, and the year to come, and Michael and I both tried hard to be upbeat and optimistic. Things would work out. I was feeling scared and nervous and excited. Yes excited, for some reason, because I wanted to prove to myself that I could beat everything that was thrown at me. I had survived a life-threatening operation and now I had to get on with my life and make things happen. Good things for me, and my family, especially my dear darling husband, who was the light of my life and my rock. 'I can do this' was my mantra as I fell asleep to the sounds of fireworks and Furby chirping under the duvet.

15
JUSTICE FOR THE LITTLE MAN

....

I have mentioned that we had been dealing with a court case. The story begins way back in 2007 when Michael was still working in Spain. He could see the way things were going in property sales and the only direction they were headed was down, so he decided that the way to approach the whole estate agency business was to cut costs, and maybe the way to do this was to save on offices with expensive shop fronts. People were becoming more and more used to using the internet, and certainly people looking for a house in Spain would often come into the office having already been online and seen what they wanted. An estate agent could soon become obsolete and it seemed more sensible to offer a more slimmed-down service and therefore operate with less expensive costs.

So Michael decided to create a back office for an online estate agency. This is a technical thing, folks, means absolutely nothing to me, but actually what they achieved has never been done even to this day. The nub of the idea being an automated system that did all the paperwork, so for example they wouldn't need a secretary to write a letter, or an email, it would all be done by the computer. When it was all up and running, the plan was to franchise the business. It was a fantastic creation and is still sitting on my husband's server to this day.

Together with his director, Andrew Jepson, and his web master, Ki Hume, the three of them started to work night and day. Basically for no money, except Ki who was paid by Michael. Every now and then Michael might sell a house and there would be funds for a while and this is where my role in the business came in. I was lucky enough to be working and wanted to help, so we used my money to keep everything going. Slowly the concept grew and we had our business plan: we'd offer cut price house deals for a flat fee of £995 which was to be paid on completion so there was no money up front. A very unique selling point. So everything was in place and going swimmingly. I was going to star in a new play, *Calendar Girls*, which was destined for the West End and possibly Broadway, eventually, and Michael spent six months working the north London area with the £995 concept and ironing out any problems that arose re the 'back office'.

Now we were ready to franchise the business. This concept bizarrely had come up in a meeting that I had with PRIME, Prince Charles's charity to help people over fifty to create their own businesses. I had been invited to St James's Palace, recently, to have a brainstorming session about this very subject, and was able to contribute one particular piece of advice to potential franchisees:

'I would like to point out here that anyone who thinks you pay for a franchise and then sit back and expect the company to do all the work is seriously deluded, and it is not the job for you. It is incredibly hard work to get it up and running, so it is not for the fainthearted.'

Riding high on the crest of a wave (big mistake), Michael and I decided to get married in 2008. Raising one's head above the parapet brought the spotlight on us and the press returned to the old cuttings regarding Michael's past, which is a little colourful. I have written about this in detail in *Lost and Found* but just to fill you in if you haven't read it (how could you not!), my husband served eleven months in prison for 'furnishing false or misleading information'. It had absolutely nothing, I repeat *nothing*, to do with property.

You'd think that he served time and that should be the end of it, but his guilty plea was to be used against him all those years later when he set up his online estate agency, Virtual Property World. A man who owned a similar online estate agency in Worcester decided to wipe out Michael and his business. Mr Darren Richards started to write about Michael and our business on a blog, using Michael's previous trial as background, and sent links to the blog to the body that regulates franchises. Please believe me I am not trying to defend what Michael did back then, and neither has he ever not accepted his plight, but the point is it was seventeen years ago, and he has never been in trouble again, and more importantly he was *never, never* charged with property fraud which is what Mr Richards was trying to claim in his sensationalist blog, posted anonymously online: 'CONVICTED FRAUDSTER MICHAEL PATTEMORE RUNNING VIRTUAL PROPERTY WORLD FRANCHISE.'

Would you use a company run by convicted property fraudster Michael Pattemore to sell your property?'

It was absolutely nothing whatsoever to do with *property*. This important piece of truth, though, meant nothing to Mr Darren Richards when he posted his damning blogs.

The other accusations levelled at us, and which really hurt me, was that I somehow would endorse something that was not straight. The actual words used were 'Virtual Property World is "fronted" by Lynda Bellingham'. I have been in the public eye for forty-five years and worked for several high-profile charities during this time that would all vouch for my honesty and integrity, so much so, if I may blow my own trumpet briefly and say, I was awarded an OBE this year for my charitable works. But Mr Richards then went on to attack my son Michael too:

'Lynda's son, Michael, appears in their home-made adverts as the arrogant estate agent, and in another of the adverts as a happy home seller [I think this shows his versatility as an actor personally!]. He also claims to be an actual franchisee of Virtual Property World.'

But that is the truth, what is wrong with that? If he had bothered to check his facts he would have seen that we made my son Michael do a National Association of Estate Agents course and signed him up to the team so he could learn a trade that he could do when he was out of work. Everyone knows how hard it is to earn a living from acting alone. The fact we did the adverts for the website together was an added bonus, we had the talent on the doorstep. But I ask again, how petty and mealy mouthed is all of this?

When we were first alerted to the blog in the midst of my *Calendar Girls* tour, Michael had a pretty good idea where the blog had come from – we were aware of Mr

Richards and his company Estates Direct which was a competitor to our own – but how to prove it, and what then do we do with the information, and more importantly stop them from ruining us!

Michael sat up all night surfing the net looking for lawyers who dealt specifically with this kind of internet violation.

Finally in the middle of the night he woke me with a start. 'I think I found someone, Lynda. I am going to call him first thing' and, boy, when Michael says first thing, he means first thing. I was awoken again from my much needed beauty sleep at 7.30 next morning to Michael dialling and pacing the floor.

'No one will be in an office now, Michael, for goodness—' But I was cut off and apparently mistaken, because Michael was now talking excitedly to a Mr John Spyrou of Pinder Reaux who was delighted to take his call.

'This is our speciality, Michael, and we will use all our powers to help you. People have no idea, as yet, just how dangerous the internet is going to become. At the moment it is like the Wild West, manned unlawfully in pockets, with the odd law maker with a gun that happens to be pointing in the right direction, but that is not enough to save so many people from destruction, especially children.'

How right he was, and as we well know it seems that every day now there is another suicide caused by hurtful words online, another bullying incident, an act of fraud, and so many general nasty people having a go. Need I say more?

We now began our investigation in earnest. I could see Michael was not going to give up until we had nailed whoever had posted these blogs – at this point we were not sure if it was the boss man.

The initial problem was to get Google to take down the blog in the meantime, because it was seriously affecting the business. Talk about stress and where I am today. Every day brought with it another heartbreak for Michael, and meanwhile I had to work every night and put on a bright smile for the public. Thank goodness for John and Rupinder, our lovely lawyers.

Once the blog had been removed we then had the next battle, which was to convince Google and WordPress to give us the IP address of the blogger so we could move forward with our case against them. Months of waiting, and more money. How many families facing the same sort of problem as us, in terms of social media and blogging and bullying, have that kind of money? Does no one have a social conscience anymore?

And then on 14 June 2012 we were granted a Norwich Pharmacal order by the high court. Sounds like a prescription for piles, doesn't it?! It might just as well have been the way we were feeling. But it worked, and WordPress was the first to confirm the IP address, followed by Google. It was enough for us to serve Darren Richards and Estates Direct with a lawsuit in the last week of July 2012.

We were now embroiled in the internet Wild West, and once Darren Richards had been served with his papers Michael got a message to say that Richards had called and would Michael call him back?

I was very nervous about the whole idea and was worried that Richards would somehow try and wriggle out of his commitment. Michael spoke to the lawyer, John

Spyrou, on the Saturday evening and John encouraged him to return the call. My canny husband did so but made sure he recorded the conversation. Thank God he did because this is where the mystery deepens.

In the telephone conversation that Michael recorded, Mr Richards professed to be dumbstruck by the news and deeply upset, not to mention completely ignorant of who might have done such a thing. However, as head of the company, he accepted it was his responsibility to his team to get to the bottom of the matter. He assured us he was seeing his legal team in the morning, and once he had all the facts and figures he would get back to us. We never heard from Mr Richards again except through lawyers' letters, which I suppose is understandable, but suddenly Mr Richards seemed to know everything about the blog and admitted it was his company that had posted it.

Writing this now I try not to feel too upset, what is the point? It was all so fishy and by the time we arrived to knock on the door of the offices for mediation, on 10 April 2013, I think both Michael and I knew we were on a hiding to nothing. Unfortunately we are not permitted by law to tell you what happened in the mediation suite, but suffice it to say it was a very long and distressing day and we came out knowing that money will always win. We wanted to go to court, we had always wanted to take it further, but we were always advised it was too risky and there would be no money in it for us as our company was so new it had no records of profit; it was all up for estimate. So yes we did get a public apology from Mr Richards and he did have to pay costs, all of which went into the fees we had had to pay out. We lost our business and I lost faith in any kind of justice for the little man. It is a cruel and harsh and unfair world. Little did I realise just how cruel and harsh until June came 'busting out all over' and I was diagnosed with cancer.

But we picked ourselves up, dusted ourselves down and moved on. Michael and Bradley have just finished a fantastic conversion of two six-bedroom houses in Muswell Hill and they will make a handsome profit which will be well deserved. We have a beautiful family and many things to be grateful for, apart from the small matter of a terminal illness. But do you know, even that is bearable, because I will be able to come back and haunt Mr Richards in his darkest hours. Watch this space!

16
ADJUSTMENTS IN THE
UNDERWEAR DEPARTMENT

....

January 2014

Here I was in 2014. That first week at home after my operation was very strange. Anybody who has spent any time in hospital and had a serious operation will remember those feelings of highs and lows. One minute I would feel exhilarated and shuffle out to the kitchen clutching my scar and make everyone laugh, and the next I would be hiding under the blanket wishing I was back in the safety of my hospital bed. It was most bizarre. With all due respect to my all male household they made a very perfunctory attempt to watch over me, and it was clear, very quickly, that things would not progress far without a shove from me: the washing and ironing, for instance. Although I have a lovely cleaner called Julia who comes once a week with her mum Maureen, they are only there for four hours and there is not time to attend to the pressing needs of two twenty-something young men who like to look smart.

'Do it yourself,' orders hubbie Michael.

'I will teach you,' I offer.

Neither suggestion seemed to hit the mark so I started doing a bit from time to time. For this I got told off, but the trouble is I can't bear living in a mess, it made me feel worse. The cooking was not going very well either, so when they had all left in the morning I would potter around making a pie, or a soup or something, for supper. This was not just for their sakes, I may add, I would have starved if I had waited for them to come and ask me what I wanted. I resorted to keeping my bedroom door open at all times so I could hear the front door, and whoever arrived would be greeted with, 'I am in here!'

I felt like Miss Havisham in *Great Expectations* shut away in my room, though hopefully without the cobwebs!

The black moments would often arrive in the middle of the night, when I couldn't sleep and everyone else was happily away in the land of nod. I could feel Furby moving about, and I was also aware of my whole stomach holding all this evil cancer inside it. It was as though a battle was being fought under my skin. I have never been able to lie on my back for long, but now it hurt to lie on either side, so I had no choice but to learn to sleep on my back. Months later and I am still not used to it, and it is so frustrating when you want to turn over and you can't.

But by the second week I was feeling so much better and, although I was still walking like an old lady, I was back at the kitchen island and feeling OK. Then I managed to pull a muscle and felt pain again, and I felt low and miserable. I had to lie down more, and as soon as I lay down my brain would take over, and I would start to think, which was not a good idea.

The bizarre thing was that I would forget that I had cancer and address the whole deal as if, once I recovered from this operation, I would somehow be cured. It was only when Justin Stebbing's secretary, Lesley, rang to make some appointments for my next lot of chemotherapy, that it hit me like a train. I still had to deal with all that.

Justin wanted me to meet a lady to go through the pros and cons of clinical trials. 'Well why not?' was our response. I had nothing to lose and a great deal to gain.

I lost two months' chemo due to the operation and the recovery time, and in six months' time I wanted to reverse the bag and go back to normal. I was back in the LOC by the second week of January and hooked up, yet again, for six hours every Friday morning from 8.30. The one setback was that I was on a new chemo which caused hair loss. So far I had been so lucky not to lose my hair, and it made such a difference to my state of mind that I was thrown completely by this news.

'But you can wear a cold cap,' advised Clare, my lovely nurse. 'It freezes your hair follicles so the chemo can't touch them. It is very uncomfortable for the first twenty minutes or so but then your head goes numb, and you can't feel anything.' Lovely!

But I took her advice and persevered. The cold cap was very uncomfortable to start with and, if you look at a photo, the hat has the effect of pulling your face down to your chest. So I reckoned I resembled a very old hunt jockey in need of a face lift – it is not great for the morale let me tell you.

I was by now getting much better at handling Furby, so my dear husband could leave that off his list of chores. I must say we did laugh at one point when he and I were assembled in the bathroom together for our bedtime ablutions. I have mentioned how unromantic it all was, and I remembered reading a book that advised young women never to reveal too much of themselves to their loved ones, that they should retain an air of mystery. Ha! Try that when you have a stoma bag. I was standing in front of the bathroom mirror with my lovely brown bag hanging off me, sporting my train tracks on my stomach from my operation scar, my various bruises from all the injections, and I was rinsing my mouth with salt water to help the sting of the mouth ulcers I now had, not to mention the invisible discomfort of thrush caused by the chemo. Romance?

However, a little secret, dear readers, into our fascinating private life, for which Michael will probably kill me. He dared to start to have a pee and I jumped up and down like a wild dervish and screamed, 'NO! Please I insist we retain some mystery. We are not allowed to pee in front of each other except under extreme conditions!'

Michael just burst out laughing and replied, 'Bloody hell, Lynda, it doesn't get more extreme than cancer!'

Enough said, I think.

So life continued, and I did start to lose some hair, much to my dismay, but it was still there, enough to make a reasonable hairstyle work. Thank goodness for Carol Hemming, the lovely lady I keep on about who is the most incredible hairdresser. She advised me on wigs I could buy, and then when the time was drawing nigh for my visit to the Palace to collect my OBE, she showed me what she could do with a hairpiece and a blow dryer, and it was very impressive. In fact, in the end, she managed to do my own hair and make me look half decent which is no mean feat.

I did go to a fabulous wig shop in Notting Hill Gate called Trendco. Just in case I needed back-up later on. I literally walked in, picked a wig very similar in colour to my own hair, popped it on and it fitted perfectly. I don't wear it when I am doing personal appearances because I feel the press will just go on about my hairstyle again instead of focusing on whatever it is I am doing.

I will never get used to the idea that I am of any interest to photographers or press. But can you believe this story? Michael and I had tipped up one Saturday morning to do some shopping at Waitrose in Finchley. We were outside the store at 8.30, nice and early, so we could whip round and get out quick. I never bother to wear make-up for these outings and I certainly would not bother to wear my wig unless it was doubling as a hat to keep my head warm. Anyway, I probably did look a frightful mess, but so what? Two weeks later I am on the front cover of one of those awful rags, *Bella* or *Woman*, looking terrible and the headline shouts:

'LYNDA BATTLES HER CANCER' or something equally lurid. Who has such a sad life that they loiter outside supermarkets to snap some ageing actress out with her shopping trolley?

A similar occurrence happened this July when I went up to Worcester University to accept a Fellowship from Lord

Faulkner. In 2013 I had attended a forum on domestic violence and met an inspirational woman called Ruth Jones. She had suffered domestic abuse and violence in her marriage and was a strong campaigner for raising the issues. She is a principal lecturer, researcher and consultant specialising in domestic and sexual violence. Ruth had also received an OBE over the same period as me, and she had asked me if I would open this new National Centre for the Study and Prevention of Violence and Abuse and receive my Fellowship from Worcester University at the same time. I was supposed to have gone to the ceremony in November 2013 but was, of course, unavailable due to illness.

In July this year Michael and I travelled up to Worcester in the morning on the train, and spent a fantastic day with everyone. Before the ceremony there was a forum attended by all sorts of people from different groups and associations, and the NHS and the police, and I gave a short address about why I supported the centre. Now I have done various things for charity hostels and refuges over the years, but I never go into any details about my own situation, which was heavily covered in the press twenty years ago now. I wrote about my marriage in my autobiography *Lost and Found*, but enough is enough, and time passes. It is not pleasant for my sons to be constantly reminded of the issues we had and, to be fair, neither does my ex-husband need to be reminded all the time. Everyone deserves to be allowed to get on with their lives.

Try telling that to these people hoping to fill the pages of their vacuous mags. I went to get my week's shopping and there is my face staring back at me from the cover of

Woman's Own magazine, with the headline: 'I AM TIRED OF BEING FRIGHTENED'.

They all know I have cancer so I presumed it was about that. Oh no, it was harping back to the break-up of my marriage in 1996. What upsets me is that someone at that conference in Worcester that day taped my speech and then sold it to the magazine. Or a journalist picked up somewhere I was doing something with the Domestic Violence Centre and just cobbled it all together. It made no mention of the positive side of the day, i.e. I had received a Fellowship and how wonderful it was that this centre had been able to exist, it just rehashed old stuff.

I was so upset I actually went on Twitter and explained it was nothing to do with me, and of course lots of my followers understood that and the way these people work, but several people replied they had only bought the magazine because I was on the front and were disappointed. So there you go, the perils of a bit of fame that one never wanted in the first place. Don't get me wrong, I completely understand it is also important for my work to get the message out there, and for that I need the media. But why can't it be kept to the subject in hand? If I have a story to tell, or a TV show to advertise, that is fine, it is just all the rubbish they then pad it out with, and if they cannot speak to you personally, they just edit things you have said in the past and call it an exclusive interview.

My next job, after restarting my chemo and sorting out my hair, was to find a suitable outfit in which to accept my OBE. It wasn't as easy as you might think, as I now had Furby to consider, and dressing has all become about disguising him. The Investiture was on 14 March, the day before my mum's birthday. How proud she would have been, they both would, my mum and dad. It is at times like this when you realise how much you still miss the people you love when they are gone, but that wasn't a thought I wanted to share with my family that day for obvious reasons. To spoil the occasion by bringing in my mortality would be insensitive. Can you imagine trotting up the red carpet to HRH Prince Charles and blurting out that it was such an honour to receive an OBE, especially as I would be dead by next Christmas so it would make a memento for the family I'd leave behind! I wanted the family to be 'up' and out and proud. A mixed bunch we were, but we had worked hard and kept it all together.

I also wanted to indulge that 'shopping' moment. I did not have to feel guilt because I was there as my duty to Queen and Country (I can make up an excuse for anything and anyone!). It was my big day and much as I was embarrassed I was going to indulge myself and enjoy it. I might even let Furby have a glass of champagne! I went to all the big department stores but there was nothing. I ended up in Selfridges, which is huge but, to my mind, so badly laid out.

What used to be so lovely about going to a posh department store was that each floor had its own special feel. There was the young and trendy, the everyday, the mature woman and the really posh designer room where one could wander around and pretend to be able to afford what was on offer. Nowadays every floor is like a flea market, with rows and rows of clothes hanging squashed together. There are designer rooms but they are terrifying, manned by stick insects, both male and female, who can hardly bear to look up from their iPads or phones to serve you. It is really depressing.

I walked up and down for at least an hour and a half and only saw one coat dress that vaguely represented what I had in mind for my big day, and that had a designer label and cost £3,000! It was just not worth spending that kind of money for one day. I needed to be able to mix and match so I could wear the outfit again slightly re-arranged. I remember Joan Collins discussing the problem with me once at a charity event. Her answer was to find a dress that she really liked, and that fitted her perfectly, and then have several made in different colours. What a canny dame she is. So I was a bit stumped.

Then I turned to the font of all knowledge, Andrea Schaverein, my friend and colourist, who knows everybody in North London and would no doubt link me up to a contact who would find me a dress. She came through good, and sent me to a little shop near Marble Arch in New Quebec Street. The lady who owns the shop, and designs the outfits, is called Suzannah. What a treasure trove of frocks. Suzannah had a rail of ready-made dresses from which you could choose and then she would make it to measure. I had decided to use a fascinator I had worn only once for Helen Worth's wedding, which was a very subtle French navy. Suzannah had a lace dress that matched exactly. Fitted, and knee length, with long sleeves, thank goodness. How difficult is it to find a lovely summer or cocktail dress with sleeves?

To go over the dress I found a white wool and silk fitted coat, with a neat little pleat in the back and turned up cuffs. It was so simple and yet so chic. I was sorted, and then Suzannah suggested I go to a shoe shop in Islington for some shoes to match my coat. Emmy shoes are located in a lovely row of shops in Cross Street, N1. Oh dear, she had some amazing shoes, mostly handmade, and completely unique. They were not cheap I will admit, but no more than the designer boys on the street. I ordered some off-white suede court shoes and a bag to match – well, it is not every day one gets an OBE – and I could wear all these items again. I was delighted and thrilled with my purchases. What I had not realised, but sister Jean pointed out to me as we left, was that the Duchess of Cambridge is a valued customer, and there was a copy of *Hello* on the seat in the shop with the Duchess sporting a pair of Emmy shoes. What can I say? She has very good taste and I expect she was thrilled when she saw me in mine in the Palace News the following week.

Underwear had become another area of interest since Furby had arrived, and it was certainly causing me more than a little grief. The trouble being, the Elastoplast effect of the bag hanging down means it gets in the way of the knicker line. OK, maybe not a Victoria's Secret knicker line, but let's not go there.

I can't imagine Victoria's Secret will ever have to consider underwear for wearers of a stoma. Though having said that, I could be very wrong, and it would be incredibly liberating and a wonderful campaign for young women who do have to cope at an early age with operations for Crohn's disease and colitis, and diverticulitis. I recently saw an article in the paper about a very brave young woman who had to wear a stoma, and she was photographed in her bikini with her accessory. I was so impressed with her bravery, and wouldn't it be great if an underwear company took up the cause and helped make specialised underwear for those customers?

I hadn't yet found anyone who specialised in this kind of underwear but I had made a useful discovery. I found some all-in-ones from Rigby & Peller which are fantastic at hiding Furby. They squash him down gently and keep him in his place when I am wearing a dress. Rigby & Peller do amazing swimming costumes as well because they are made on the cross and hold and lift and, believe me, they are so tight nothing can escape. Again, they are not cheap but to know I am covered and safe is worth paying the extra.

The final touch underneath the dress and the underwear are the tights. I bought these Spanx tights which have a reinforced gusset, don't you love that word? Gusset! If ever Furby was going to think of making a run for it (pardon the pun) these would halt the progress immediately. So I was completely covered, God willing, for every eventuality.

17
A GRAND DAY OUT

....

The big day was such fun.

I had received the letter from the Cabinet Office in November 2013: 'The Prime Minister has asked me to inform you, in strict confidence . . .' I couldn't believe it! I was so thrilled to be recognised. I had to keep the secret until New Year's Eve, no less. It was torture and I didn't even tell the boys because they might inadvertently post it on Facebook or something. It never ceases to amaze me how everyone has to tell the world everything about themselves these days. I expect more from my children, who should know better, but they are all the same!

While I was in hospital over Christmas I almost forgot all about it until suddenly, as I was preparing to leave the ward for the operation on 13 December, someone mentioned the New Year's Honours List, and I realised with a jolt that it would feature me.

I had some wonderful letters from family and old friends and even strangers. The boys were so thrilled, which was lovely, though we did have a little family joke about how it was a shame I had to get cancer to get an award. I hasten to add it was not true because I am told that the application had gone in long before it was announced I was ill. In fact, it had come about thanks to the efforts of my friend Katie Mallalieu. Katie was a primary school teacher at the time, and had been to see *Calendar Girls* when we were in Manchester. I had shown her around backstage and she had become a friend. We discussed all sorts of things, but one thing we both agreed about was that we wanted to help get Alzheimer's out to the public. I was an Ambassador for the Alzheimer's Society because both my adopted mum and my birth mother had suffered with the disease.

I worked as an ambassador for the Alzheimer's Society and I cannot tell you how much things have changed for the better in the last five years. I managed to visit several care homes and was really impressed by the attitude and care of the people involved. We hear so many negative stories in the press, and I understand there are some terrible things that have happened in the care industry, but at the same time there are people doing marvellous work as well.

In 2014 dementia has finally been recognised fully by the government, and the UK is leading the way in treatment and understanding of this dreadful disease. But a few years ago when my mother died of Alzheimer's it was still a hidden illness. People did not want to talk about it, and my poor father used to be ashamed of my mum. Many of her friends deserted her and she could not understand what she had done wrong. We were very lucky and found her an amazing home in Stone, near Oxford. The staff were all so loving and caring towards the residents but it makes such a difference having that awareness and understanding of the condition now. Those visits around the country taught me so much.

As well as my charity work with the Alzheimer's Society, I also worked for Barnardo's too and while I travelled the country, touring with *Calendar Girls*, I spent a lot of time visiting outreach homes for young single mums. These outreach homes are twenty-four-hour houses of safety. I went to one home in the middle of a building site near Bradford and it was such a shock to someone like me from a happy middle-class family. The windows were all boarded up but the lady who opened the door to us was so warm and welcoming. There were girls as young as twelve and thirteen, some already mothers. They were wary and suspicious at first, but as we sat down to tea and biscuits they relaxed.

The shocking thing was their attitude to Michael who had come with me. They seemed to flirt with him in a very knowing way. It was the only behaviour they knew in front of men. Two girls, who were sisters I discovered, had both lost an eye. They had been gouged out by their pimp to keep them from running away. I will never forget their beautiful young faces marred by those gaping holes. How many of us, safe at home, have any idea what kind of world there is out there? I had such admiration and respect for the women and men who work day and night to help these young people and restore their lives to some kind of normality.

I am so grateful for having the time to visit so many different kinds of charitable organisations and it taught me so much and humbled me. My life as an actress in the glamorous capital was a far cry from the real world.

Katie and I began to work together regularly in our joint efforts to raise awareness and money for the cause of Alzheimer's. Katie organised a walk up in Lytham St Annes for her school and I went along to start them off. Katie had worked so hard to organise the event and we were very disappointed with the local press who were less than enthusiastic.

The next project was to create a calendar of photos and paintings of real people with dementia next to a famous person that had links with dementia. Katie came to Manchester again when we were touring the following year, and took photos of me and her as a starter, and then Lisa Riley agreed to do one, and several of the *Calendar Girls* supported us. I organised a little PR launch down at the Athenaeum Hotel in London. Richard Barber, a friend who is a well-respected freelance journalist, wrote a piece for us, and *Yours* magazine, who are always so loyal, also did a piece. Sadly sales of the calendar did not soar and Katie had used her own money to get them made, so I was feeling really guilty. However, Katie is not a young lady to be deterred and she continued to organise all sorts of things to raise money for the Alzheimer's Society.

We met again in Bradford 2012 while I was doing pantomime. I had had a text from her then boyfriend explaining that Katie had been having a really rough time, and gone through a personal tragedy, and would I ring her and try and get her to come and visit. I was only too happy to be able to return a little of the kindness and support she had shown me and my good causes. We met for lunch and had a long talk. She had, indeed, been through a good deal of heartache but she was and is a fighter, all credit to her.

We met several times while I was up in Bradford, and on one of these occasions she arrived with a huge pile of paperwork.

Katie explained she had proposed me for an Honour, and it was required that the proposer assembles all manner of proof of the work, and the reasons why they thought their candidate should be accepted for an award. There were pages of stuff from every charity I had ever worked for, it seemed, and what they had to say about me. I was incredibly touched that Katie had done this and gone to so much trouble. I did not share her confidence that it would get her anywhere and, to be honest, did not give it another thought. How wrong could I have been?

A year later and we were all off to the Palace. I was able to take three people as guests but I cheekily rang the organisers and asked for four, as my stepson Bradley, who lives with us, would have been left at home and that seemed a little harsh. I so wanted to share this moment with my family. I was unable to get a place for Michael's daughter Stacey, which was a shame, but she made me feel less guilty by explaining it would be very difficult for her to make babysitting arrangements. So with Stacey unable to come, it was me and the lads!

They all looked amazing in their suited finery. Michael had declared very early on that we had to drive to Buckingham Palace as the last time we were there, for a garden party, he had just loved driving through the main gates and parking up in the quadrangle where all the coaches line up at state occasions. It is very exciting, I must admit, to be able to walk up the steps into the palace and remember all the times one has seen this scene on television. The problem was his beloved Range Rover – the pride of his life, though some might go as far as to venture the love of his life, sad though it is – only had two seats in the back. When Michael bought the beast he decided he wanted the special big seats instead of the standard three. So now what would we do? Undeterred, he rang Range Rover in Somerset and asked if we could borrow one for the day with the three seats. Not a problem, was the reply, so now we were all piled into a white Range Rover Sport winging our way to the Palace. The boys tweeted and took selfies the whole way, it drove me mad! Then I succumbed and tweeted a photo of my hat. I know it is ridiculous but I couldn't help myself. We were hysterical as we swung into the courtyard and parked up.

When you have accepted the invitation to attend the ceremony you get all sorts of different leaflets and instructions about the big day – I must say the organisation is phenomenal. You can even buy a DVD of the day, filmed with your family as they walk through the palace, and sit in the ballroom, and watch the ceremony. My lot looked like they were casing the joint! One rather special advantage which comes with the Honour is that you can use the OBE Chapel in St Paul's for marriages and christenings. The lads were very keen on that.

'Yes, it would be wonderful if you could all find a wife and have children in the next six months, because that may be all the time I have left!' I said. 'Highly unlikely though,' I added realistically.

When I talk like this it might sound rather crude and insensitive, but the written word is sometimes so different to the tone of a sentence when spoken. Sometimes I do something like this deliberately, just to remind the boys of what is going on. I don't want them to spend every day depressed and overpowered by a sense of doom, but if I can just keep it light enough to nudge a reminder sometimes I think it is positive, otherwise we might all push it so far out of our minds that when the day comes it will come as a terrible shock once more. I don't know what to do sometimes and that is the honest truth. All our hearts will be broken whatever is said or not said.

Once inside the building the boys admired the artwork while I went in search of a toilet as I was very concerned about how Furby was going to behave. I was so excited and very nervous which, as we all know, tends to affect one's normal habits and Furby was no exception! I started forward to find someone who might help me and was lucky to be addressed by a lovely Palace official who showed me the way. The loo was packed with ladies in every style of hat and fascinator you can imagine, and all talking ten to the dozen. I duly queued up and I quickly realised there was going to be a problem as there was no disabled toilet and I needed a basin. I have promised myself I am going to be completely open about all aspects of this awful illness, so do bear with me as I fill you in on the mechanics of a stoma bag. Those with a weak stomach should turn the page now!

When I empty my stoma bag, it is very difficult to point it in the right direction and often the toilet bowl is too far away to execute a clean manoeuvre. So I decided on my own little system using plastic jugs which I can easily place on a side in a toilet cubicle or bathroom somehow. I empty the bag into the jug, wash the jug out and away we go! Unfortunately, if I am not in a disabled toilet I have to risk popping out of the toilet when no one is around, and performing the jug washing ceremony before anyone comes in. Standing in the loo in Buckingham Palace I realised there would be no chance to pop out to an empty basin. So I decided the only way was to kneel down and empty the bag straight into the bowl thus also avoiding any mishap. God forbid I missed and my beautiful white suede Emmy shoes were tarnished in any way! So there I am folks, on one of the most important days of my life, kneeling in a public toilet, albeit Royal, emptying the stoma. You couldn't make it up!

My variety of jugs, though, have proved very successful. Dear sister Jean went on a hunt and I have three different sizes to suit different handbags. Darling, it is the 'must have' accessory these days. I often get rude looks and tutting from people when I come out of the disabled toilet in restaurants, and long to lift up my skirt and say you don't have to be in a wheelchair to be disabled! It is these kinds of things that make me a better person, because now I can understand so much more, from so many different perspectives, and hopefully as people read this they will also think about what is going on around them. Life is a battle for so many of us and I just wish we were all a little bit kinder to each other.

Having sorted myself out I was ready for the fray. I said goodbye to the boys at the top of a very impressive staircase as they were being taken to the ballroom, ready for the ceremony to begin, while we recipients were taken to the long gallery to be instructed in our bowing and curtseying. The atmosphere was buzzing. We all looked so lovely in our finery. I bumped into Katherine Jenkins who looked amazing, and we exchanged a hug. A few years previously she had bought my old house in Muswell Hill. Small world, isn't it? We were politely told off for stepping out of line by a lovely young Palace official, as we had been carefully placed in a special order in lines so that there would be no mix-up when we arrived at the platform to receive the medal. If one stepped out of line, disaster could strike! We went through the moves . . . two steps forwards, bow or curtsey, accept medal, quick chat, and then two steps back, turn and walk.

We were informed that today's Honours would be given to us by His Royal Highness Prince Charles. I wondered if he would remember me as we had met several times recently with PRIME, and I had had the embarrassing encounter with the nice man who wanted to meet Prince Charles and gatecrashed my conversation with the Prince. We were led, in our lines, through the ballroom, where I spotted my party sitting staring at the ceiling, through another beautiful room and down a long corridor to wait on the side for our names to be called. The lady next to me was a very distinguished professor of urology but she surprised me by asking me if I would show her how to curtsey. Well, red rag to a bull, asking an actress to show you a move. We had a practice, and then suddenly I heard my name and nearly keeled over in my panic to get to the door. I entered the ballroom downstage left, so on my right were the audience (the guests and their families, and further back empty rows of seats which would eventually be filled by the likes of us as we returned to the ballroom).

On my left was a wonderful array of dignitaries. I had no idea what they all did, but it was a bank of colour, with the gold of the braided uniforms, and the reds and blues and silver of the extraordinary amount of adornments that were on display. Behind the rows of Palace officials was a huge arch and a statue, I seem to recall. The whole room had enormously high ceilings and the gold filigree, and painted stucco, and the red carpet and the chandeliers just made everything feel unreal. As I stood in the doorway I could see across the ballroom into the next doorway, and beyond that the next, golden light stretching as far as the eye could see. I had the same emotion of excitement and awe as when I received a coronation gold coach from school to commemorate the occasion. It was a tiny replica coach in gold, with the white horses attached. I used to turn it over and over in my hands, lost in the magic. Now here I was stepping onto the immaculate red carpet and walking slowly to the point I had been told to stop and wait. A very impressive gentleman was on my left and whispered that I would turn and curtsey when I heard my name. All well and good, but the man struck up a conversation with me!

Did I like the Palace? How did I feel?

I wanted to say to him 'shut up I can't hear my cue' but I think instead I did a tiny shush to him because it was true I couldn't hear very well. Suddenly I heard 'Bellingham' and turned and curtseyed and walked two steps forward.

Prince Charles did recognise me and gave me a lovely warm handshake. 'Lovely to see you again, Lynda, and we are so pleased you have been awarded this honour. How do you find the time to fit everything in?' he asked, as he leaned forward and placed my medal on a little hook which was on a clip that had been carefully placed on my coat. It makes everything so smooth for the hand-over.

'Much like you, sir, with difficulty,' I replied. 'However, the good news is that now I can sport an OBE people will take me much more seriously, and I will be able to raise much more money for charities, Yours included!' He laughed and stood back, which was my cue to take my two steps backwards and turn to the right and move off at a regal pace towards stage right.

Once out of sight of the ballroom you are then whisked to a table on which all the boxes are laid out, and yours is found and your medal placed inside. The whole operation rolls like clockwork. You then walk to the end of this small corridor and you are back in the ballroom, once again, and placed in a seat for the remainder of the ceremony. I knew this was going to happen and I knew there was another hour to go, so I asked permission to make a detour and turned left to the loo, just to be absolutely secure. I had the room to myself which was lovely and spent a few minutes holding my medal to my chest and gazing at myself in the mirror with a big grin on my face, silly cow.

After the final award had been given we all trooped out into the quadrangle for photos. I had pre-paid for my shots as, once again, the organisation of such things had been so efficient. I had filled in a form weeks before and now all we had to do was follow the leader and do as we were told. There was a rather lovely moment when a lady who had been awarded an MBE was explaining to me that the choir that she coached had come down to cheer her on, and would it be possible to have a photo? We walked to the front of the Palace to be greeted at the railings by these girls singing away, their voices soaring above the traffic noise of a busy London day. All I could see was a row of shining faces and behind them banks of tourists waving their cameras in the air. Talk about multicultural; the world was right there on the Queen's doorstep.

I had arranged to have a lunch at The Delaunay restaurant in the Aldwych. Chris Corbin and Jeremy King are the owners, and they have been part of my London life for thirty-four years. We had first met when they were managers of Joe Allen restaurant in Covent Garden, owned by my dear friend Richard Polo. I was introduced to the place by Christopher Biggins, naturally. We were a gang of actors making our way up the ladder and Joe Allen was our watering hole. It became known as the actors' restaurant and people would book tables just to watch the actors. Its success, in the early days, was mainly due to the fact that, believe it or not, one could not get a decent meal after ten at night in London; incredible to think that a city like ours was so parochial.

Richard worked so hard to gain the trust and affection of the theatre world and then the rest followed. If one was appearing in a play in the West End there would always be a single red rose delivered to the stage door. So many birthdays, deaths and bar mitzvahs have been celebrated there. The piano player, Jimmy, would bang those keys into the early hours. I remember going to have supper when Elizabeth Taylor was in town and gazing at her as she sat in a discreet corner having her supper. I can tell you her eyes really were violet and so beautiful. I met Lauren Bacall one night, who took a fancy to my ex-husband which was interesting. There were suppers too with Liza Minnelli, Christopher Biggins, Joan Collins and Percy Gibson, her husband, who all have very wicked senses of humour. Richard Polo did not allow customers to approach famous guests while they were eating, which was fair enough, but I remember one day sitting at the table next to Edward Fox who had just been playing the King of England and an American lady managed to seat herself next to him. She was beside herself with excitement.

'I can't believe, I am sitting next to the King of England,' she cooed.

Everyone tried to tell her Edward was just an actor, including Edward, but she was not having it. In the end it was easier for all concerned if he just played the game. A waiter arrived to escort the fan from His Majesty's presence, and Edward bade her farewell in his best voice saying, 'Goodbye, dear lady, we wish you health and happiness.'

He gave her a little nod and she curtsied!

An evening spent at Joe's that sticks in my mind more than most was during an event organised by Sir Cameron Mackintosh, for the Royal National Institute of Blind People, in 1988. The Queen is the patron and her presence was expected at this one-off night of entertainment at the Lyceum Theatre. It was to include all Cameron's shows over the years and also all the actors and actresses he had worked with and that, amazingly, included me! I had been in Cameron's first professional tour that he produced. In fact I nearly married his brother Robert after that tour. When Cameron handed all the cast of *Hey, Mr Producer!*

a mug at the end of the evening to say thank you, mine said on it: 'To think we were nearly practically related!' For this charity event, a scene had been devised to include all his leading ladies through the years singing 'Hey, Mr Producer!' I was lined up with the likes of Julia McKenzie, Siân Phillips and Sue Pollard. We were a motley crew!

It was so scary to be in a line-up like that. During the course of two days we were all called to hang around in case we were wanted onstage. I didn't care about waiting around, I would wander from dressing room to dressing room star spotting. There were so many names and performers and dancers that everyone had to muck in and share dressing rooms. They were full to bursting with costumes and wigs and screams of delight. I had a magic moment meeting Hugh Jackman in the corridor, and we chatted about *Oklahoma!* which was the show he was doing at the time. Not only is he incredibly handsome but so very nice as a man.

The actors and dancers all used Joe Allen as the watering hole-cum-green room. It was so weird to see the restaurant full of diners from the city, in their suits, alongside dancers sitting on stools at the bar, with practically nothing on, doing the splits from time to time. I was sitting having a coffee when in came Clarke Peters, well known for his wonderful performance in *Five Guys Named Moe*. Another handsome devil may I say. We spent the morning telling theatrical stories and laughing a good deal as I remember. Imagine my surprise twenty or so years later when he pops up in *The Wire*!

By the time the show was to start I think everyone involved was completely exhausted. But that is when

Doctor Theatre takes over, and as the curtain rises and the lights hit you, you feel like a sunflower tuning its face to the sun. I spent most of the evening in the wings just watching great talent. At one point I turned to the man next to me and whispered, 'Isn't this wonderful?'

'She is out of tune,' he replied. I turned in amazement to find I was facing Stephen Sondheim!

Early that afternoon I had sat at the back of the stalls and watched my hero perform. The orchestra had gone for a tea break much to everyone's dismay. They could not be persuaded to wait, and as they have a very strong union there was no discussion. I personally think that it is a sad state of affairs when for such a unique show – which is what this was – they could not stretch the rules. Of course we have to be protected from overzealous employers who would work people beyond endurance, and I have been in theatres where we worked all night to get the show ready, but that is part of the magic. Anyway, the orchestra went for tea and left this wonderful actress to sing her solo without musical accompaniment. There was just a spotlight on her as she sat very still and started to sing. I hope she will not mind me saying this but her singing is not melodic, as such, but it is full of emotion and her consummate performance as an actress turned this solo into five minutes of magic I will never forget.

Dame Judi Dench I salute you.

So Joe Allen's is tied up in good memories with fond friends from my theatre days. We all had some fun times together over those years, and now Chris and Jeremy from Joe Allen's and the great Mitchell, their general manager I think his title is, are my benchmarks for good food and good taste and loyalty, and so I wanted to go to The Delaunay for my special lunch.

The Delaunay has a private room at the back of the main restaurant. It has a long line of windows so every now and then one can look out and see what the world is getting up to. I had invited several friends such as Biggins and his partner Neil, Peter Delaney and Paul de Ridder, David Pugh and Dafydd Rogers, and my literary agent Gordon Wise, and Sue Latimer, and my very old (she will not like that, but we do go back forty years) friend and flatmate and first agent Felicity McKinney. Katie Mallalieu was there, of course, and dear friends Angie and John Chandler and my brother-in-law David with his partner Carole and my old mate Nickolas Grace. Linda Agran, the delectable Mrs Scott, was present, and last, but by no means least, my sister Jean. It was so hard trying to decide who to invite because I wanted everyone I love to be there but we just couldn't afford it! I can't remember why Lynda La Plante was absent as she is another very important person in my life; I know we invited her.

As I write this I am only too aware of just how many people were left off the list and I want to take this opportunity to apologise and suggest it had nothing to do with how much I love you, but the limitations of time and space and money. But in that room, oh my goodness, practically everybody made a speech and I was rather embarrassed! As the wine flowed, so did the love. I couldn't eat a thing but kept taking gulps of champagne either to fortify myself or to stop the tears from flowing. When the celebrations came to an end, Michael ordered two taxis because there were a few of us going back to North London. I have to admit I got in my car and immediately thought I was going to be sick. I clung to the handle and looked straight ahead the whole journey home. I couldn't speak in case I threw up and my lovely driver, another Michael, was chatting away to me about my day. I felt terrible.

I managed to make it up to our apartment and realised I was all alone. The boys had gone out, taking advantage of their groomed appearance, and Michael was in the other car with Angie and John. Probably gone to the pub I thought grumpily, how dare my husband desert me in my hour of need? I was transported back to my student days when too much cider induced this terrible drunken torpor of sickness and self-pity. As I lurched round the flat getting undressed I was talking to myself, whining about how nobody loved me, and it was my big day and now I was drunk, and all on my own, and how the hell do I get this dress off by myself?

I did one very sensible thing though, folks, I removed the white suede shoes immediately. Just like in the loo at the Palace, the protection of these shoes seemed of the paramount importance. Just as well, because seconds later I was standing in the middle of the bathroom, barefoot, surrounded by poo. Furby was obviously so disgusted with my behaviour he had rebelled and burst! Picture the scene, I know it is not very pleasant, but one has to see the funny side, as Lynda Bellingham, OBE, crawled around on her hands and knees mopping up the mess. Twice in one day on my knees in the toilet, people would talk! I was in floods of tears, not so much about being ill and the cancer, but because I had let myself down and realised, yet again,

I would never be in control of my life or my body. What I did learn from this episode was I certainly did not need to make things worse by giving Furby too much to drink.

By the time Michael came home I was in bed supposedly fast asleep. He thought I was, because he crept out and went and slept on the sofa. I fell asleep still complaining to myself that my carer had dared to let me down and go to the pub in my hour of need. And before you say to yourselves, what a cow, it was her own fault, when I woke up the next morning I was mortified and gave him a huge big hug because in all seriousness it must be so hard for Michael sometimes seeing me ill, and he handles everything brilliantly. He deserved a night out in the pub with his mates, God bless him.

So my OBE day was memorable in many ways, not all of them pleasant, but that is the story of my life as you have probably realised. Nothing seems to quite go right, but I am determined to enjoy the good bits for as long as I am here on the planet.

18
CENTER PARCS WITH THE FAMILY

....

A year previously it was coming up for my sixty-fifth birthday, and our fifth wedding anniversary, the weekend of 31 May 2013.

'Michael, let's do something special to celebrate. I would love to take the whole family to Disneyland Paris for a long weekend and we can celebrate when we are there,' I said. By the whole family I meant my two boys, Robert and Michael; Michael's son Bradley and his daughter Stacey and her husband, Sam, and their two boys, Cooper and Oakley, aged seven and four, and my grandson Sacha aged three. In my ignorance I reckoned that it would be cheaper than flying everyone to Orlando or Florida. Silly me! It would roughly work out to about £15,000 for four days!

It was time for Plan B. There is another place that is my favourite for children and adults and it is full of happy memories for me and my boys: Center Parcs. We decided on the Longleat Center Parcs because Stacey lived down that way, and it also meant we could all visit the lions at Longleat on one of our days there. We booked and were all set to go.

As there were so many of us I decided to be ahead of the game and take all my own meat and supplies, and pick up all the extras in a lovely shop they have on site. It's a lovely shop but a bit pricey for a full grocery shop. So we stacked the back of the car with enough meat to feed an army for a week, same with the wine and beer and cold drinks, and at the last minute I had bought a beautiful chocolate mousse cake with Happy Birthday and Happy Anniversary written on it, which was carefully lodged between two boxes to keep it safe. The boys followed in their cars, and we would link up with Stacey when we arrived. We had spared no expense and got three villas, because Stacey and her family needed space, none of us wanted to share with the lads, and Michael and I like our own time. We would play all day and do barbeques at teatime, but then we needed to sit and chill on our own veranda and watch the sun go down together. Well, hopefully there would be sun to watch.

All the villas were a mere bike ride away from one another. Don't you love the bike riding? For anyone who has not had the pleasure of time spent in a Center Parcs, let me tell you, it is all about riding a bike. The moment you have unpacked your car you have to return it to the car park for the remainder of your stay, and either walk everywhere or hire a bike. If you have not ridden one for a while it is a little daunting as the nice boy wheels out your trusty steed. You pray no one is watching as you mount up and – assuming you are lucky to stay on the first time – wobble your way out of the hire shop round the corner into a bush! It takes a while to get used to but as they say 'you never forget' and soon you are speeding up and down the hills, ringing your bell like a mad fireman.

The first night was the actual birthday/anniversary. We had married on the day of my 60th birthday. I had booked a table in one of the many restaurants at Center Parcs and I had delivered the cake in its box, to be opened at the appropriate moment. We had a lovely meal and then I beckoned for the cake. Nothing happened until a few minutes later and a very upset-looking waitress asked to speak to me privately. I left the table and followed her into the kitchen where she opened the box and showed me, not a beautiful cake, with candles flickering, but a round choc-olate melted pile of . . . !

'I'm so sorry, Madam, but we have only just opened the box and found it like this,' she whispered. 'We can put candles on another cake for you but it won't have the message written on it, obviously,' she added, as if I couldn't see for myself the disaster of the situation.

For a brief moment I wanted to scream or cry, but decided life was too short and said, 'OK, just bring another cake with some candles.' Which they did, and the little ones loved it and the big ones understood. Silly Granny should have known it might melt in the back of the car and certainly should have refrigerated it when we arrived. However, there was no use crying over spilt milk or even melted mousse and it did not spoil a wonderful evening.

As we all strolled out of the restaurant, feeling pleas-antly lubricated, it dawned on me there was no getting into a taxi nor a slow stroll up the road, it was a bike ride home. Oh my goodness. Now comes the bit where one has to pedal hard to keep the headlights on, never mind get up those hills you flew down on, and negotiate the lovely wooden flyovers with a drop on one side. We had to fly through the forest, so beautiful and cool in the daytime with so much foliage spreading over the bikeways, but at night it is like a scene out of Harry Potter and I am desperately watching this way and that for giant spiders! I am trying hard to keep up with the children, who are loving every minute, and practically home and in a bath by the time Michael and I are approaching our road. Of course, he has been playing macho Granddad, and pedalling like a lunatic, but I notice not always in a straight line!

'Here we are,' I call out to his backside disappearing further into the forest. 'Michael, you have missed it, our villa is here.'

I start to dismount and hear a crack and then a whispered 'shit' and then silence.

'Are you OK, dear?' I shout into the darkness. There was a pause before a small voice says weakly, 'Yes I'm fine.' I wait a few moments and there he is, the Bradley Wiggins of Somerset, wiggling towards me, stubborn to the end.

'You missed the turning,' I announce with glee. 'Bit the worse for wear, my lover?'

'Not at all,' says he, and tries desperately to get the bike into its railings and lock it. 'I just missed the number in the dark.'

I left him to his manoeuvres and his wounded pride.

By the following day we were all in the groove. What is so great is there are no cars to worry about, so the little ones are relatively safe, except maybe from the bigger kids on bikes showing off, and indeed some of the adults too! We

Where are the crackers Dad?

And guess who
made the gravy?

The two nurses who looked after me,
Grainne on the left and Michelle on the right.

I wish I had worn my wonder bra.

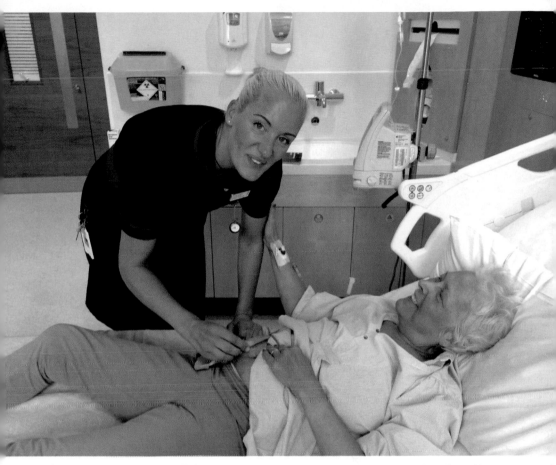

Rebecca Slater, queen of the Stoma bag. How can someone so lovely sell one something so ugly and enjoy it! Never too posh to pooh.

My birth father,
Carl Hutton.

My second cousin Nikki
Pittman with her family.

The family resemblance is astonishing. On the left is my father as a baby and on the right is me at a similar age. Below is my father as a young boy and on the right my grandson Sacha who has such a likeness for his great-grandfather.

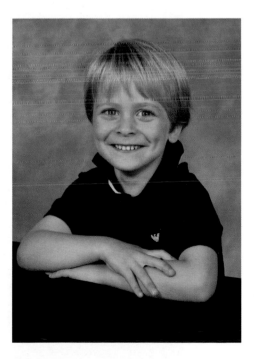

Me and my lads at Center Parcs 2013.

My dear sister Jean and I celebrating her 60th birthday.

Fatherhood for
my son Michael
Peluso and my
grandson Sacha.

Granny and Grandson
Sacha on my precious
Cockington Rocking
horse.

Me and my love, Michael. This photo was taken by Brian Aris for YOURS
magazine and he very kindly let me use it for our 2013 Christmas card. Just
hours after it was taken I was rushed to hospital with severe abdominal
pains which was the start of the decline to Christmas and my life-saving
surgery. It is amazing what make-up and hair can do for a girl!

all did our own thing. I was straight into the spa, which was heaven, and left them all to it. Come teatime the fire building began, and there we had three young studs, Michael, Robbie and Bradley, and Sam, a man who had done three tours in Afghanistan, and my husband. Oh my word what a man-fest of testosterone! It was less of a barbeque and more of a bonfire but it kept them happy all night. We laughed and played with the children and we all seemed to be tired at the same time.

Suddenly everyone was gone, and Michael and I were alone in the forest, sat in front of the burning embers, watching a duck waddle across our veranda and a lone blackbird, I think, serenading us. It was magic. This was a routine we pretty much repeated for the next two nights until it was time to pack up and say goodbye.

Now would be a good time to tell you about my grandson, Sacha, who I had time to get to know a little better in those few days. My son Michael and Kate, Sacha's mum, were together a good while. They always had a stormy relationship but I do think they loved each other. Although one always hopes this will be enough, it is not always the case, and so they sadly split up and not too amicably. They then tried a brief reunion and Sacha was the result.

Over the last four years I think both Michael and Kate have had to do a good deal of growing up. Once a child is born it is no longer about yourselves, everything must be about the child. I was still on tour for almost all of Sacha's first three years and some of you reading this may criticise me for maybe not being more hands on. I know a lot of my friends who just could not wait to be grandmothers

and now spend many hours of their days being childmind-
ers. That may be fine for them, but I was still a working
actress providing for my two sons and my stepson. Michael
and I had got married when I was sixty, our intention was
to pool our resources and try and spend the next few years
– while we were still able – building up security for us in
our old age. Neither of us had any kind of pension, apart
from a state one, and that was not going to go far, so that
is what we were doing.

In my head I knew my son did not have the wherewithal
to support a child, as he was a struggling actor, so I would
try and help him, and in turn Sacha, in other ways. We did
not see Sacha much at all in that first couple of years and
I do regret that time lost, especially as now I am running
out of time. However for the last year-and-a-half Michael
sees him every other Sunday, and brings Sacha round for
Sunday lunch, and gradually we have made friends. Center
Parcs sealed that friendship, I like to think.

It is ironic that suddenly I had so many plans for outings
in the summer holidays, only to be told, a month later, that
I had cancer. It has been a hard thing to deal with and I
know my son sometimes feels he cannot always cope with
the future and fatherhood. But I know he will, he has to,
that is what a parent does. Forget one's own fears and
troubles and get on with making a life for your children.

It was the thought of the effect it would have on my children that stopped me contemplating suicide in the months
after I left their father. I had a pretty rough four years after
my divorce. I was a single mother for those eight years,
before I met Michael, and they were difficult years for the

boys. Boys need a father, and not a parent who is angry about their ex-wife, or the way their life has panned out through no fault of anybody but themselves. I threw myself into work, which I was forced to do as the only breadwinner, and I had a great friend and a wonderful companion/assistant in Alena. Alena was a girl who had come back into my life after several years, she had struggled against the odds with a boy a year older than my youngest Rob. We all helped each other through those very dark hours.

The one thing I tried to hold on to at all times was a line of communication between me and my boys. It is the weirdest thing sometimes, and it must have happened to some of you reading this, that when your children are behaving so badly in front of you and you are struggling to teach them right and wrong, manners, the importance of education and to keep away from drugs and not drink too much, the tasks just grow into huge unassailable peaks. The desire to give up and hide under the duvet with a bottle of vodka, or take up smoking again, do look preferable.

But I was too old for all that and I knew I had to stick with them and practise what I was preaching. They might not have appreciated it then, the little sods, but surely one day I would hear the words 'Thank you, Mum'. I managed a fair amount, and what I found out since, over the years, I am so glad I did not know at the time! Yet I must say that if they ever went anywhere to stay with other families, or a visit to a relative, the report always came back to me that they were lovely, well-mannered boys. Better that than the other way round I guess, and never being invited again.

When I was in my fifties I would still pour everything out to my parents. I talked to them about everything. They died within a month of each other, just after Christmas 2004; I was devastated and felt like an orphan. They had always been there for me. I realise now how much anguish I must have caused them all through my twenties. I used to ring late at night from some party, too much the worse for wear, and beg my dad to come and find me. He always did, God bless him. They watched me go through two disastrous marriages and never judged me. I am just so sad they never met Michael because at least finally I have got it right. It took me sixty years but some of us are late developers in common sense. At least my dear parents were spared seeing me go through cancer.

I like to think my boys and I are still open and honest with each other, but obviously there are things I don't always get to know straight away. Michael split from his most recent girlfriend, Senel, over Christmas 2013, while he was doing pantomime in Wolverhampton. Separation is the most challenging thing to deal with in a relationship, and my son did not handle this one very well. So suddenly he was back on a sofa bed at our house, not something my husband encourages! Still we all managed to get through three months without a row, which was something, and then Michael got a room in a flat with a mate from school.

Both of my boys are trying very hard to stay positive in front of me I know, rather than pour out their latest troubles, and my husband encourages them to do that. I appreciate his thought and care for me, but it is hard for me to make my husband understand that he must not entirely take away that relationship I have with my boys. That is how we survived when we were a family on our own. That is what I had with my parents.

So my boys and I, and my lovely stepson Bradley, and hubbie, all sat down initially after the diagnosis and had a good cry. The prognosis then, back in July 2013, was much more positive. Since the operation in December it had lessened considerably. But once we had managed to absorb the blow we all carried on much the same. It is the power of the human spirit not to dwell all the time on the problem. We all forget as much as we can, and then suddenly something might come up about an event in the future and we are plunged, briefly, into despair once again.

I did feel very strongly about what I wanted them to take from my death, other than feelings of loss and abandonment, and that was to be inspired by my energy. I have struggled this last year to accept that I am going to die before I have finished everything I set out to achieve. There is so much I wanted to explore, not least to have some life with my beloved husband. We had such plans to go to China and Japan and Australia this year. We love travelling together and we laugh so much. None of that is possible now. I wanted to do the play *A Passionate Woman*, and give David Pugh and Dafydd Rogers and Kay Mellor a huge stonking great hit and myself the satisfaction of showing the world just what I could do, given half a chance. I wanted to achieve an Oscar for playing the perfect old lady in a big motion picture – albeit a cameo role, I know my place – and pay Hollywood back for treating me so shoddily as a young actress. After doing all that I would then have been able to sit back by choice and only do the stuff I really wanted to do, and spend the rest of my time writing blockbusters, sitting on the terrace of a beautiful Georgian house, in Somerset, sipping my own homemade elderflower cordial. It's not much to ask for, is it? Ha! Well as the song says in *South Pacific*, 'You've got to have a dream, if you don't have a dream, how you gonna have a dream come true?'

So all this energy to go to waste? I don't think so. I have told Michael and Robert that much as it will hurt to lose me they must pick up the banner and do it for me. Get the most out of their lives and go for it. No procrastinating, they must take my courage and use it. I do actually think, in one way, losing me will help them move forward in the next phase of their lives.

Bradley is very fond of me, I know, and I rely on him to keep an eye on his dad. I know my husband is going to be in a bad way for some time afterwards, and I want all the boys and Stacey to rally round. Not that Michael will ever admit weakness and will probably want to hide away, but at least they will be there if he needs them.

So that is my legacy to them all really, if you feel like giving up or lying down under the duvet, don't you dare, because I will be round every corner haunting you, with the inimitable words, that crop up all the time in our household these days: 'Stop yer whingeing, at least you haven't got cancer!'

19
WHEN I AM GONE

....

April–May 2014

Although I was now on an even stronger chemo I was determined to get out and about. My first engagement was lunch with my youngest son Robbie at his place of work. He had recently joined the Mandarin Oriental, a super five star hotel in Knightsbridge. The restaurant there is Heston Blumenthal's flagship after his very famous restaurant The Fat Duck at Bray. I was very excited at the thought of a Heston adventure, but just as chuffed to think my son thought me cool enough to have lunch with in public! The hotel was absolutely magnificent, and I was old enough to remember when it was called something else entirely, like the Hyde Park Hotel, and royalty stayed there. The dining room has long windows all across the restaurant so that diners can look out onto Hyde Park and people watch. It seemed to me that every time I had just put something juicy and full of fat in my mouth, a stick-thin jogger would pass by clutching his or her bottle of water. Life is too short as I very well knew by now, and nothing was going to stop me indulging myself, except maybe the prices on the menu in front of me.

'Don't worry, Mum, I get 25 per cent off because I am staff, have whatever you fancy.'

I checked the wine list which was of bible length and discovered there was not a bottle of wine under £50.

'OK, you pay the meal and I will treat us to the wine, is that a deal?'

He nodded and then we were suddenly given a glass of champagne by Paul, the lovely manager.

'A belated Mother's Day gesture to you,' he smiled.

'Well, thank you so much,' I said. 'I was just about to order this bottle of Brunello, what do you think?'

'A very good choice, Madame. Robert, I can see where you got your good taste. Enjoy your meal.'

What a charmer! Robbie and I were both glowing with the compliment.

We had a beautiful meal and tried to order different things so we could share. There were pink luscious duck breasts and belly of pork, with perfect accompaniments, and the wine was amazing.

'Don't have too much, Mum,' advised my sensible son. 'We don't want a repeat of the OBE day, do we?'

We had such fun people watching. So extraordinary are some of the creations that come out of the kitchen that there were several Japanese tourists taking photos of their dinner. I chose tipsy cake for my dessert, which is a very old English pudding, and it was exquisite. I might suggest Mr Blumenthal try bringing back cabinet pudding again.

But the surprise at the end of the meal, and only someone like Heston Blumenthal could think of this, was to bring out an ice cream trolley and watch the waiter make you a mini ice cream cornet with nitroglycerine. It only takes five minutes to freeze the mixture and present you with a perfect cone of yummy ice cream, topped with sprinkles of your choice. It was a fantastic finale to a perfect lunch, and I was so proud as I walked out on the arm of my beautiful boy. That day will stay with me until I die.

Again, time rears its head and decides just how many more such moments I may have. I am trying to make sure that every occasion is enjoyed, every Sunday lunch, every birthday. Spontaneity is very important, because it is too easy to make plans and stick to them rigidly when sometimes it may be better for all concerned to go with the flow. In the last few weeks I have begun to feel that maybe I cling too hard to 'plans' especially because they make me feel secure. Doing the same things creates a sort of timetable and pattern to everyday life but actually it is not always very satisfying.

A couple of weeks ago we were coming back from a chemotherapy session, as usually we go straight home and have dinner and go to bed. But that night as we were passing a very popular pub in Highgate called the Red Lion and Sun, I noticed they were advertising fresh oysters and a bottle of Pinot Grigio as a suggested evening meal. I know how much Michael adores oysters so I shouted 'STOP!' loud enough to be regarded as an emergency procedure and we parked up and had a fantastic night out. We rang our friends Angie and John, who live round the corner, and sat in the garden of this delightful hostelry with them and joined several random customers in having a boozy Friday night out. The useful thing for Michael is that I rarely drink now as Furby gets a little overcome, so he can drink away and I can drive us home.

Talking of moments, I have been having quite a few with big son, Michael, in a professional capacity. A friend of Michael's, called Donna Taylor, wrote a short film called *Too Close for Comfort*. It is a great little story, and she asked my son Michael if I would consider playing his long-lost mother. It was a case of life and art getting mixed up once again, but I was delighted to help. We filmed a couple of scenes and I thought no more about it. Then a few months later Donna rang to say the film was getting huge amounts of hits on YouTube, like 9 million! Would I be prepared to make some more?

By this time I had been diagnosed with cancer and not feeling my best, but a job is a job, and if Donna could work round my chemo days I told her I would be delighted. We roped poor old Jean in because we needed her kitchen as a location, and Donna being the true pro wrote a script involving my character having cancer. Some of the scenes became very emotional – it was hard enough to play that role but the storyline was all too real for me, it was my life – but it was a joy to work with my son. He is certainly starting to find his feet as an actor and all he needs is a break. I often have a little chat to God these days and suggest that as he has decided to get rid of me could he please pass on any good luck going spare to my sons!

I was never a pushy mother. Because my parents were quite easy-going about my education I have been fairly laid back about all of that as far as the boys go. However, they often accuse me of not having been tough enough with their educational requirements. Honestly you can't win can you with these bloomin' children?! It used to be a nightmare trying to get them to do their homework and the coursework and I did once succumb and do my eldest son's essay for a history of art exam! I must confess that looking back I am just glad they are well mannered and not in jail. That's a joke by the way . . .

I am sad I will not see who they marry, or live with, because for all they say now that they don't trust relationships, I know in my heart they have so much to give someone who will unlock their dreams. Sometimes I think it is easier for me to understand my stepson Bradley, because I am slightly removed from him. He too has proved a joy and I just so want them all to be content within themselves.

At the beginning of March poor Justin had been trying hard to be positive, but I could see in his eyes that things were changing all the time. The lovely ladies on the frontline hinted that maybe now was a good time to put my house in order and think in terms of months. My biggest worry is that my sons have a roof over their heads when I am gone. Michael and I have discussed this so many times in the last few months. But then we have had to discuss everything about our lives. I read somewhere that 75 per cent of couples never talk about death together, or their wills, or financial state. This is a huge problem and a minefield.

About five years ago I wanted to make a documentary about everything to do with death as so many of us, especially women, find themselves not only grieving for their beloved, but having to face a mountain of paperwork concerning the running of their lives. In my mother's generation it was even worse, as running the home and paying the bills was regarded as completely the man's domain.

My parents were very advanced and far seeing about such things, and spent many months investigating the financial ins and outs of death duties and life insurance and inheritance tax. My dad hated the inheritance tax – don't we all? How can the government be allowed to tax us twice? Why shouldn't we be able to leave our hard-earned money to our children if we want to? Nowadays our children simply have no chance of getting on the housing ladder without help from their parents, and some of us just do not have the ready money to help. I was incredibly lucky to receive a gift from my hermit Uncle Percy, down in Devon. None of us thought he had a penny! That money became a deposit on a flat, and a foot on the rung of the property ladder. Needless to say I would be rich today if I had not had to give half of the sale of our house to my second husband and bought him a restaurant. Still the past is the past.

The point I am trying to make is that it is vital as couples that you get everything out in the open from the start, and don't let our very British dislike of talking about death get in the way. I wanted the documentary to be informative and fun, which I realise is an odd concept to many people, but I felt I could pull it off. None of the broadcasters wanted to know, unfortunately, as they thought it would be too morbid, and now, because recently Billy Connolly did one which was less than successful, and Channel 4 are showing one about people with terminal illnesses, they feel there have been enough.

But they are missing my point about how we approach death and prepare for it, be it financially or spiritually or just waiting to die, which too many people do. They get to retirement age and seem to stop. Why for God's sake?! Medically speaking, your chances of living to eighty are very good. Obviously the quality of your life is important, and I do think that just because the medical stats say you could live to eighty, too many people somehow see it as their right. Doctors are not magicians and Nature is tops when it comes to deciding when our bodies have had enough.

Because of what has happened to me I feel I am in a position to talk about death with some authority now. I accept I am going to die in the next few months, weeks even. This is a piece of string moment, I know, but it came up in terms of treatment a few weeks ago when the colon specialist, Richard Cohen, was talking about reversing my stoma. Professor Stebbing made it quite clear that if I stopped having chemo I would probably last eight weeks, and in order to reverse the stoma I would have to curtail chemo for the operation, so that kind of says it all.

I can accept this, and the good thing about dying this way is one can make a plan. I have to put aside all the emotions and concentrate on practicalities.

There was a wonderful moment last year when Michael went down to Somerset to visit his dad's grave. It is a beautiful cemetery on a hill with gorgeous views. Anyway I get a text from my husband with a photo of two mounds of earth next to one another and the message: 'Saw these and thought of you and me. They are on offer, two for the price of one, so I bought them, isn't that great?'

Only my husband . . .

But in a sense it is better to address the problem sooner rather than later. Like my parents, my sister Barbara, who died in 2008 of lung cancer, used her last six months to organise the family finances. And she organised her funeral, which was lovely. The interesting thing is, though, does one choose a funeral with hymns and prayers that suit only the deceased person? Surely part of the mourning process, and that includes the wake or the funeral, is for the loved ones left behind? Should they not be allowed some say in the proceedings? Michael thought it would be great for our friend Peter Delaney to come down to Somerset and conduct the service there and all my friends could troop down also for the funeral.

'I wouldn't expect everyone to have to come all the way down here to pay their respects,' I said. 'I want a tribute or something that is nice and handy, and anyone who fancies coming in and saying goodbye can do so easily, not to have to get on a train for three hours.'

'I bet they would do it though,' said my lovely husband.

'That is not the point. I do not want to put people to a lot of trouble. Couldn't we have a family ceremony in Somerset, if it is your wish to have me buried down there, but maybe we could organise a memorial service in London for friends, and anyone who wants to call in, and then have a party afterwards? That is what I would love.'

He looked at me askance, but I know he understood what I was getting at. I will suggest some hymns I love, and maybe some readings, but I will not insist that the boys, or my sister or nieces, should feel they have to read or sing or anything like that. It is a tough call. We have reached a compromise, I think, and there will be a service in Somerset and a knees-up in London! So if you are passing, do drop in for a quick boogie.

As far as the finances go there are things one can try and do, but ruling from the grave is a moot point. One tends to think that a will cannot be changed but I have been involved in two cases now where that is blatantly not true.

I remember a wonderful moment when I was travelling with all my family to India just after I had tried to commit suicide, and was still married to my first husband Greg Smith, God rest his soul. He was a lovely man but a terrible husband. I knew when I married Greg that there were problems but, like every woman in the world, we all think we are going to be the one to change them, don't we? I cannot believe this happened to me but I had an unconsummated marriage. Apparently it is quite a common problem. Greg could have one night stands where he felt no respect for the woman in his bed but as soon as he fell in love he was unable to make love. I was the second wife, Cheryl Barrymore was his first and one has to feel for her, poor woman. Going from Greg to Michael Barrymore! I think Greg married four times in all and never found the happiness he sought.

At the time it was incredibly hard to deal with because he always made the woman think it was her fault. I talked to Cheryl about it once and she agreed that it left her feeling useless and unattractive and it was the same for me.

When I told my parents my father could never get over it. 'You are trying to tell me that Greg never wanted you?' He would ask the question over and over. 'I just can't understand the man. Good Lord that is what marriage is all about, Lynda. You poor girl, you do all the housework and cook and clean and look after the bugger and he can't perform. That is your reward for goodness sake for being a loving housewife!'

Oh my dear old dad. Anyway, they were amazing about my insensitive and desperate call for help, and once we had all recovered they decided we would all go on a big adventure, possibly the last one ever as a family, as we were all grown up, and would not be able to take advantage of Dad's discount with BA for much longer.

Just as we were rolling along the runway and gathering speed to take off, Mum said, 'Have you made a will, Lynda?'

'No,' I replied, wondering if she knew something I didn't about the plane!

'Oh dear, just think if this plane crashed, all our money, and all our homes, and the farm would go to Greg as he is next of kin at this moment!'

I couldn't imagine a worse-case scenario. The thought of hitting the deck and seeing Greg with the keys to my mum and dad's house as I closed my eyes and kicked the bucket was horrendous. But it could have happened.

The only way to truly keep money safe and make sure it goes into the right hands is in a trust, but that is a nightmare for most of us and it can be very expensive. One should write a will, and make sure you have people around you trust to keep an eye on it after you are gone. The worst and most common scenario has to be if your husband or partner meets someone else.

I would hope, in a way, that Michael does meet a lovely lady, who could look after him and they could have a loving relationship. He says he doesn't ever want that again, and I understand, but things can happen. However, if that lady was on the lookout for a meal ticket, and decided that my sons' inheritance was of no consequence, that once I was gone they could fend for themselves and she and Michael could sail off into the sunset, then that would be a disaster. I want to know to the best of my ability I have them sorted. It would be just the same the other way around as well. So my dear husband has been running round like a mad man getting everything straight, and I do recommend that anyone reading this (God, I hope there are a few) will take note and make a will.

And while we are on the subject, a living will. Here is another thorny problem. I do not want to be resuscitated after a heart attack or a stroke, thank you very much. I am not going to try and tackle the whole issue of assisted suicide here, but it is a subject one should think about very seriously. It is so hard for me to discuss this with the family because we are coming from some different places. In a way their arguments are purely selfish. They want me to live, obviously, and so do I, of course, but if that is not possible then please let me go in as dignified a way as I can. I don't want to be remembered in a bed, out of it, on morphine. I look at myself now on a bad day, haggard and drawn, with my white hair flat against my head and a stoop of tiredness and pain, and it is so depressing! I do not want Michael and the family to say goodbye to me looking like that. I see their faces now when I need to lie down, and I catch them watching me with such sadness in their faces. I want to say goodbye as me, Lynda Bellingham, B to my husband, Mum to my boys, Bellie to my friends, Lynda Bellingham OBE to my enemies!

Funnily enough I went to a psychic recently who opened the conversation with, 'You have many people who hate you, Lynda.'

What?! I haven't noticed that particularly in my life. If I have ever had run-ins with people I have tended to ignore them or just avoid them.

'A lot of negativity in your life and you have had to fight very hard for anything good to happen.'

Now that is true. People talk about how lucky I am and I can honestly say that is not the case. I have made things happen by sheer force of will and I have refused to be overcome by other people's negativity, such as that of my second husband. I have always looked to the future and moved on, but luck, as such, has not been in abundance and certainly not at this point in my life. But the idea that there are people around me who hate me was quite a shock. However, I do not have the time to worry about them now; if envy was ever a cause I am sure they feel better now knowing I won't be around much longer!

I wasn't gone yet though and I was continuing to try and get out and see people as much as possible so my next outing after my lunch with Robbie was in April to the Lady Taverners Spring Lunch. What a group of ladies they are! Over the years I have made some very good friends with these campaigners and while having a good time they raise thousands and thousands of pounds to buy buses for children with disabilities, and help them with facilities to play sports and have great days out. Each charity has a different approach to raising money and the Lady Tavs is like joining a club. You get to know people over the years and it is lovely to all meet up at these functions and have a gossip.

In May I attended the Alzheimer's Society's Dementia Friendly Awards, and once again bumped into all sorts of different people I have seen over the years getting to grips with this insidious disease. Great Britain is now a leading voice in Europe, along with Holland, and even throughout the world. Japan has a huge interest in its ageing society and dare I say it has a much more respectful approach to the elderly than some parts of the UK. But slowly we are coming to terms with the illness and dealing with it. However there is so much research that still needs to be done that money is vital, as usual.

Thankfully the Alzheimer's Society is getting there and we have Dementia Friends, supported by Prime Minister David Cameron. Hopefully we are teaching society a whole new way of approaching sufferers. It may be naive of me, but I hope that attitudes towards all the vulnerable members of society will improve through this campaign and we as a society will take time to consider those around us. In terms of care, of course, we have a long way to go. The government should have an all-party policy on this. We all know what it is going to cost in the future and it should not be a political issue. I feel that the NHS and caring professions have to be addressed and the public need to accept that they will have to pay towards their healthcare.

Lynda Bellingham

I think a lot can be done to educate people too. Why not make caring a decent career for a young person? Train them properly, show them it is not all about old people and nappies, pay a decent wage and make them feel an important part of the healthcare of this country. I know we hear so many awful things about healthcare but I really do believe that care workers should be given proper recognition and respect and money for the jobs they perform. They are invaluable to the running of any institution, be it a hospital or care home. God knows we are going to need more and more as the elderly population grows and there are so many young people needing work.

Nurses should be made to feel more special too because it does take a special kind of person to dedicate their lives to others. But nowadays everything has become lost in pay scales and administration and agency nursing. Carers, healthcare workers and nurses should all be recruited and young people enticed into a career with the offer of decent wages and lifelong commitment. Let us make it a profession to be proud of alongside the nursing profession. I now know, more than ever, just how important these people and the jobs they do are.

20
TIMES, THEY ARE A-CHANGIN'

....

June 2014

With all the recent enquiries into sexual abuse, and the Yewtree investigation, I was asked to take part in a programme about life in the seventies and how much things have changed. I must say, looking back, it is amazing just how different attitudes are now. I left drama school in 1969, and so much of my career was formed from 1970 through to the early 1980s. That part of my career saw some good, some bad and even some *really* bad stuff in the form of my comedy work, which I naively imagined was showing people how versatile I could be when in reality it pitched me into what is now known as the 'tits and arse' brigade.

Almost every photo of me in a comedy saw me either playing a nurse with big boobs or as the only girl in the programme, always wearing a low-cut T-shirt or some such nonsense. At that time women were there to be mocked and ridiculed and yes – I am afraid to say – touched up. I remember a very famous comic saying to me, 'Now in this scene I am going to drop a pencil down the front of your dress and then I look for it.'

He then spent a good five minutes basically abusing me. I just stood there not quite knowing what to do and then turned to the room and said, 'How funny was that then?'

They all looked embarrassed I am pleased to say. But the line between what was acceptable or not was obviously in a different place back then.

Of course there are serious questions to be asked about certain people and obviously there are real sex offenders out there, but some of these cases now, I think, are way over the top. Do we honestly believe that all these young bands say to their groupies, 'Now, how old are you and does your mother know you are here in my hotel room?' I don't think so!

I do blame the parents, because they really do not know where their children are half the time and they must know that if their daughters go out with not much on they are in a certain amount of danger. I can remember my dear old dad, who was so gentle and shy, telling me to understand the male psyche. As he put it, 'All men have a basic animal instinct that women do not have, and if a man has not seen a woman for some time, or indeed never, as in some cultures, to suddenly be accosted by the sight of legs and thighs and breasts is just too much for them and they attack.'

I think some of the very liberal thinkers among our female society should take this onboard. I am not saying any young girl deserves to be raped or abused because of how she dresses, but maybe a little thought and understanding of the opposite sex might not go amiss.

But back to the seventies and I did have quite a few embarrassing moments, especially if there was a bed scene. I always dreaded these sorts of scenes as they are so cringe making. I had one with an actor much older than me and I was playing his mistress and we were supposed to be making mad passionate love. We both wore knickers but I had no bra on . . . 'Intrinsic to the scene, dear' is what they always told you. Anyway the director called action and this dirty old man stuck his hand between my legs. I let out a yell and the director shouted, 'Cut!'

'What on earth is the matter, Lynda?' he asked impatiently. I looked at my co-star who was smiling at me. Smiling!

'Nothing, sorry, let's go again,' I said as I settled back under the covers.

'Action!' cried the director, and with that I grabbed the actor's crotch and squeezed, hard!

It was his turn to let out a yelp and the director called, 'Cut. What the hell is going on here, you two?'

'Nothing,' we said in unison and indeed nothing did happen from then on. That is the way to deal with dirty old men.

To be honest it all depended who you were working with. Dear Robin Askwith spent his life on those *Confessions* films trying to protect the very actresses he was being asked to abuse. None of them seemed to mind much! My first husband was the producer of the films and he used to receive large photos of so-called actresses with nothing on except a big grin on their faces, saying 'All producer's requirements will be met'.

You could be forgiven for wondering who was abusing who!

In the seventies, every time one had to do a publicity shot it was inevitably a tits and arse number. Not that I ever took my clothes off for the newspapers, but the photographer would always ask you to undo one more button or stick your chest out. That was humiliating, but sadly in those days it never occurred to me to say no.

I do regret the jobs I took on in those days and I do wonder how much it affected my career, but it's too late to think like that now. I should just be grateful I will never be asked again! Mind you, it is only two years ago that I stopped taking my clothes off nightly in *Calendar Girls*.

Doing it for *Calendar Girls* was so liberating though, for all of us, and it was not as if the audience saw anything, it was just between the actresses. Although one memorable night in Glasgow, when I had to move upstage to stand at the top of the imaginary hill and encourage the other ladies to strip, I had to take my top off and turn to the audience with my arms strategically crossed over my boobs. In order to get into that position, though, with my back to the audience while I got my bra off, I was very exposed to everyone in the wings. There were supposed to be rules about no male stagehands backstage during this part of the play, but this huge hairy Glaswegian had somehow managed to creep in and when I noticed him at the side of the stage he was waving at me, and giving me the thumbs up with a huge grin on his face, and I could do nothing!

Oh yes, there were all kinds of un-PC behaviour back in the day, but at least everyone on a Benny Hill show or a *Confessions* film didn't pretend it was anything but what it was, whereas in the theatre it was quite a different kettle of *poissons*! They try to pass all sorts off as 'art'. I remember doing a play at the Oxford Playhouse called *Diet for Women* which was loosely based (very loosely!) on Aristophanes' play *Lysistrata*. It was a great cast of women, including Lynda La Plante – then known as the actress Lynda Marchal – Lesley Joseph and Jenny Logan. We all had to wear huge rubber breasts painted blue to emphasise our femininity. The director was Greek, and very flamboyant, if you take my meaning, and kept coming at us with cans of blue paint. He then decided we also needed rubber bums so we had these enormous rubber globes tied to our backsides. It was awful and you have never seen a stronger group of women reduced to tears!

I also had the pleasure of appearing in a musical in the West End about the life and loves of Toulouse-Lautrec. Very artistic, I thought. Again it was a cast made up mainly of women with Toulouse-Lautrec at the centre of the action, played by Henry Wolfe, who did look extraordinarily like him.

We all played lots of different parts and one of my roles was as his mistress, Suzanne Valadon, who liked to embarrass Toulouse-Lautrec in front of his mother. So there was to be this scene where his mother came for tea, and while they were sitting at the table Suzanne would enter, completely naked, and start looking for something on the table, leaning across the mother in a very obvious way, as you can imagine. When Toulouse-Lautrec demands to know what she is playing at, Suzanne replies innocently, 'I am so sorry to disturb you, my darling, but I am looking for some fig leaves I made earlier, which I am wearing tonight at the fancy dress party you are giving, and if you remember correctly, we were going as Adam and Eve. Ah here they are, you have been using them as table mats.' And with that I sashay offstage with the fig leaves.

It was a funny scene and very unexpected, but oh dear, the thought of complete nakedness was daunting, and apparently had never been seen on the Queen's Theatre stage in Shaftesbury Avenue. The owners and producers were very nervous about the whole thing and wanted to see a taster of the scene before they committed to it being allowed at all. So I had to do the scene cold in the old Brixton Astoria, which was where we were rehearsing, just before lunch on a Friday. I have never been so scared. I went to the pub and had three large brandies and then went back and did the scene with aplomb! Of course everyone loved it so I was stuck with it. It never occurred to me to ring my agent and protest because I knew they would just find someone else.

Every night during the run I would queue up in front of the big mirror in the wings, where we all checked out quick changes, and give myself the once over before I went on. It used to take the audience at least thirty seconds to realise I was naked and then I could hear the whispering going round the audience. My poor father, on the opening night, asked my mother to tell him when I was about to come on naked and he just hung his head and closed his eyes! One night the stage door man called my room and said I had a visitor. Always a bit of a worry as you can imagine when you are doing a part with nakedness. I went down to the stage door to be greeted by a very elderly gentleman in a beautiful tweed suit and cape and deerstalker hat and a silver-topped cane.

'I am so sorry to bother you, Miss Bellingham, but I wanted to congratulate you on your performance and also ask you a rather personal question, if I may?'

'Fire away,' I replied.

He paused and sort of stuttered out the line, 'Do you have help from wig creations?'

It took me a moment to understand what he was referring to and it was only when I caught his eye wandering to my nether regions did the penny drop!

'Oh no,' I said trying not to laugh, 'I just ruffle it a bit!'

That's showbiz, folks, everyone a winner!

So yes I suppose one could say things have moved on since the seventies but, to be honest, the nakedness is much the same as ever, perhaps even more so, I would say.

It was fun to do the programme and remind myself of my legacy. 'What legacy?' I hear you cry. What indeed, but I do hope I will be remembered for something a little more interesting than gravy!

21
MY BIRTH FATHER

....

An extraordinary thing happened yesterday when I sat down to write this chapter, a very important chapter and, because of the way I have been writing this book, it will also be the last one I finish. I went to make a cup of tea in the afternoon and turned on the telly to catch the news. I was reminded that it was 4 August 2014 and one hundred years exactly to the day Britain declared war on Germany, at eleven o'clock that night. I returned to my desk to start writing about my birth father and realised that he was with the National Guard serving overseas from 21 June 1916 until 19 May 1918. How weird that I should start his story on such an auspicious day and that my father, Carl Seymour Hutton, about whom I know nothing really, was part of the Great War. My wonderful adopted father, Captain D.J. Bellingham DFC AFC Bar, played his part in the Second World War too.

As I was having to face up to the fact that I was coming to the end of my life, somewhat sooner than I'd ever imagined, in my prime with a husband I adore and a family I love dearly, I was drawn once again to how my life had begun and where I had come from.

It had taken me over two years to pick up the research on my real father. I don't know why I had this reluctance to do so, though I think I was quite badly hurt by the way things ended up when I had found – and then lost – my birth mother.

Years ago I went in search of my birth mother Marjorie Hughes; it seemed the right way round to do things. I suppose instinct tells you that the mother is the one to find, but looking back I now realise for me it was absolutely wrong. After Marjorie died in February 2012 I was very upset by the fact that nobody in her family wanted me to attend the funeral, and did not tell me she had died until it was too late for me to get there. I remained a shameful secret forever, even beyond her lifetime. I suppose for a long time I had felt that I didn't want to set myself up for another fall. I had a very loving adopted family who I adored and maybe I was just letting myself in for heart-break if I delved any further into my birth family. My sister Jean, God bless her, was as upset for me, I think, and after discussing the problem with her daughter Martha, they decided Martha would do some more research into my family.

There was very little to go on except a ship's log of passengers going to New Zealand in August 1947. The ship was called the *Rangitiki* and was used to carry American widows to New Zealand to meet the families of the servicemen they married or were engaged to during the war. My mother's name is there and so is my father's, she as a passenger, and he as a member of the crew. I remember Marjorie telling me about this handsome man she met onboard on the way back to the States. She had a photo of herself that he supposedly took of her, though she was not allowed to take one of him. Once back in New York she was completely smitten by him and they had an affair. She then returned to Canada to tell her parents she was going to get married. Discovering she was pregnant she rang Carl and broke the news, only to be told that there were plenty of other men on that boat and he questioned how she could be sure the baby was his.

When I heard this sorry tale I was full of righteous indignation and pronounced my father as a rotter, but now I have mixed feelings. I have discovered a thread in my heart that had nowhere to go and finally after sixty-six years I think I know where it ties up!

But I am getting ahead of myself. I didn't know what to expect when Martha started to look online but after some digging, lo and behold, she found me a second cousin, a girl called Niki Pittman. We have since done a DNA test and are indeed related as second cousins. Niki's great-grandmother was my father's older sister Berthe. Niki wrote to me:

I was born and raised in Rupert, Idaho – population just over 5,500. You don't realise what a unique culture small towns have until you move away. I never felt like I fit in there. I was an energetic competitive girl who lived in a place where women were supposed to take a back seat. I was always curious about my ancestors in Europe.

I think it is fascinating that this is a girl writing about life now in Middle America and not a hundred years ago! Though I can see where she is coming from, and I agree about the culture of a small town in somewhere as vast as the States. In the UK we mostly come from small towns and villages but they are still always reasonably close to a city. We have a handle on what is going on, but for a girl in the middle of nowhere it must have been stultifying. However, Niki used this desire to find out more and set about discovering her roots. There was an old doctor's bag in the shed full of photos and many of the answers to her questions.

Suddenly a whole new side of the family opened up to Niki, who began to research her family history in some great detail. Her great-grandmother's family were home-steaders. They travelled over a thousand miles from the only home they had known, to move to Idaho and set about establishing a home and farm. Government made land available and a family would have to file a claim and then work the land for three years. There was little irriga-tion to deliver water to the land and many mistakes were made not only by the new settlers but by the engineers in charge. It was a very hard life.

Meanwhile Niki discovered the artistic side to the family too, and it is a side to the family of particular interest to me given the career path I have followed. Another of Carl's sisters, Leona Hutton, was a silent film star. Between 1913 and 1916 she made over fifty films – lucky cow! My father also had a niece called June Clyde who was a fairly success-ful actress, and came over to Britain for a period and made several Sherlock Holmes films. My sister has managed to get me videos of these films. It is also bizarre that I have a framed set of cigarette cards in my study of film stars of the day, and there is June Clyde among them! I'd always thought it funny as I grew up that no one else in my family had shared my theatrical side, but suddenly I had a theatrical pedigree after all.

So after lots of digging by Niki and my niece, here we had my father's family. There was my grandmother and grandfather Hutton and six children, of which Carl was the youngest and Berthe was the eldest. There was fourteen years between the two of them and between them there were three more sisters and a brother, Richard Ray. As the years went on it seems that Carl had less and less to do with his family, and they really knew very little about what he got up to in his life. The one person he seems to have remained in touch with is Berthe, which we know from some intermittent postcards. And yet as a baby I think he was adored and spoilt by his sisters and very much the centre of attention.

When Carl returned from overseas he went back to St Joseph's where he had spent his childhood and worked as a welder in the same firm as his father. According to a family Bible, he married a lady called Helen Kasper on 19 April 1924 in Chicago, Illinois. Niki thinks they had a son called Jackie as there is a photo of a baby, and it was taken in Chicago and sent to Uncle George and Aunt Bertha, with the message 'love Jackie Hutton aged three and a half months'. Niki says the handwriting is the same as Carl's. There appears to have been another child born four months after their wedding – but later the birth certificate of a third child states the first child has died but Niki can find no details. By 1930 a census shows that Helen was claiming to be a widow and living as a boarder in rented accommodation with her son Jack. As we now know my father did not die until 1959, one can only assume that Helen had her reasons for not telling the truth.

Niki thinks the son, Jack, ended up in California, where he died in 2003. I could have found him and met my half-brother, how weird is that? Jack married a Phillis Hesson in 1950 and they were married for twenty-odd years before they divorced in 1970. Niki wrote to her to try and find out more about what happened to Carl. Phillis responded to say that she and Jack were married for twenty years. They had a son who died from cancer at the age of forty-one and he was childless. Jack and Phillis divorced in 1970 and his mother Helen told Phillis that Jack had moved to Hawaii and married a Japanese woman with whom he had a daughter. That was the last that Phillis heard. She told Niki that Jack didn't know his father at all and that Carl's family didn't approve of the marriage and persuaded Carl to end it.

So, folks, I may also have a Japanese niece in Los Angeles. Niki has an old address but nothing current, though there is still a house in the area in Jack R. Hutton's name. Niki wrote to the address but has not received an answer. She has discovered a new address in Hawaii for Yumiko (my niece) but no phone number as yet. This story could run and run, unlike mine, unfortunately.

As Niki has said at the bottom of one of her emails: 'Carl led an unusual life and I believe he kept almost all of it a secret from his family. I think there is so much left to uncover!'

*　　*　　*

So the question has to be asked now, what is it about Carl that has set me off?

As Niki has said when she first saw photos of him, there is something in Carl's face that is captivating. He looks like a sort of James Cagney character, the cheeky chappie who is hard to resist but not likely to give you a happy ending as a woman in his life. He was obviously doted on as a child, and I get the feeling that he inherited the theatrical genes as much as his sister Leona. But was his life a disappointment to him? Niki says she only talked to one person who ever met Carl, and he was a young boy at the time, maybe eleven or twelve. He told her, 'He was a great storyteller and told me about a gold ring that he wore made from gold he had prospected for in Alaska. I got the feeling my mother and grandmother tried to keep me away from him.'

Certainly he seems to have told different ladies different stories and there is evidence amongst all the paperwork that he had gone by several different names. But why, I wonder? There is no evidence he was a criminal. He spent the last ten years of his life in New York working in security for the government, it says in a newspaper article, but then we all know the newspapers always write the truth! It actually says on his death certificate that his occupation was custodian which is another way of saying caretaker.

So everything seems to have two sides, nothing is quite straight with our Carl. But suddenly he came to life for me because, as I was sorting the photos, I laid his childhood picture next to one of my grandson Sacha and it was like the flash of a camera. The two of them as children look almost like twins. It took my breath away to see a replica of my father Carl three generations later! The interesting thing with family is we only ever see exactly what is put in front of us at the time.

'Oh, he looks just like his father,' we coo as the new baby is presented to us, or 'she is the spitting image of her mother'. But think of the actual gene pool. Two lots of grandparents, and parents, not to mention the secrets!

When my sons were born they looked exactly like their father (thank God!) but then as they have grown they are a mix of both of us. Facial expressions are picked up unwittingly in families. When I discovered Marjorie, my birth mother, I tried hard to see a resemblance but it was difficult, and to be fair she always said I looked like my father. As a child no one ever guessed I was adopted because I looked so like my sisters but I put that down to nurture over nature. My parents were such a strong influence on us, and family was so important to them, we were imbued with that spirit of love and family from day one.

But now I am suddenly faced with a whole other side. My real father lives on in the eyes of his great-grandson. What would he have made of me I wonder? Now I long to talk to him, to show him what I have achieved. Though maybe he wouldn't want that because I have such a strong feeling he let himself down in life and would not want the reminder of his failure.

It was clear that there was an awful lot of love from his sisters and I couldn't help but wonder what he must have felt when he left America for Europe. Did he worry about being killed in action or was he looking for a rush in the thrill of the battle? Over the last few days as I have written about my father, there has been so much discussion about what happened to our brave soldiers in the First World War and what the men who fought in the war thought and felt, and the thing that most impresses itself upon me is that so many people have said their loved ones never talked about the war when they got back. I remember my father, Donald Bellingham, only once recounting how he felt when he went on a bombing tour. He was trying to explain to one of my boyfriends I think about death and fear, and he confessed that he had been excited. Yes his mouth went dry with fear as he climbed into the cockpit but it was a positive fear. He was doing something positive, fighting for freedom, and he was determined that he and his plane would beat the bastards!

He admitted though that one had to make oneself feel like that a bit just to be able to get up there in the clouds and go for it, and I am sure we can all understand that feeling. By contrast, however, years later something came up about the war and he just sat there with tears rolling down his face. He couldn't talk about it.

Carl's sister Leona (the silent screen star) wrote her brother a poem and it was published in a local paper. It is heart-rending in its expression of love for her brother. It makes me wonder if perhaps his pursuit of women was to rediscover the kind of love he received from the likes of his sisters when he was young. It must have been very hard to return from Europe to a new world but with the same old work prospects. What were his dreams, I wonder? I don't imagine he dreamt of ending up a welder in the same factory as his dad.

This is Leona's poem:

Lynda Bellingham

A Sister's Prayer

Written to my beloved brother, Carl S. Hutton, serving
God and his country in France.

God pity Women – the Mothers most,
When the world's at war, and the fighting hosts
Must take their Sons, the heart of their hearts,
Oh – God it is pitiful when they must part.
The sweethearts will miss them,
Some will be true;
But there is another, God, and I loved him, too.
I am only his sister, older than he,
But his boyish troubles he brought to me.
Sweethearts would fail him, life wasn't worthwhile
'Till he came to his sister, and she could smile,
Then sweethearts forgotten and that laddie knew
That a woman loved him, with a love
That was true.
I can't reach him, God, he is 'Over there'
YOU take my message, YOU are everywhere.
Tell him I am waiting and praying too,
That his dear feet will trod the paths ever true.
He will be tempted, God, his soul will be tried,
But I shall be waiting, my heart open wide,
Filled full of love, and joy, and pride.
Though the years may be long, or his dear body maimed,
His sister is waiting, her love the same.
Please give him that message, God,
It's just from me,
A sister's prayer entrusted to thee.

I cannot imagine that my father can have been such a bad man to have inspired such a poem. Weak, maybe, and disillusioned, but not bad. When I look now at a photo of him in his uniform, a cheeky grin on his face and these incredible eyes, I keep expecting him to wink at me!

He died young at sixty-two, just as I am going to do at sixty-six. Is he trying to get me up there with him to make up for all those years he never communicated with any of his children? I say up, it could be down, couldn't it?!

But in the meantime, I have one more thing to do and that is to write to the father I was never able to know and hope to change his legacy a little, from the sad and lonely death on a gurney in Bellevue Hospital, Manhattan, on 22 December 1959, to the head of what is hoped will be a long line of strong and fulfilled Hutton men, with a good sprinkling of Italian seasoning to boot!

A letter to my unknown father

August 2014

Dear Mr Hutton, or should I say Father? Dad? Mystery man? Everyman,

My name is Lynda Bellingham and I was born in Canada in 1948. Your name was not on the birth certificate but there is ample evidence that you are my father and Marjorie Hughes was my mother. Perhaps you remember her? She was one of your conquests on the good ship *Rangitiki*. I get the feeling it wasn't an unusual occurrence.

Please don't think this is going to be a letter of reproach, far from it, it is by way of setting the record straight in my head. I have neglected you too long, and now that time is short and I have so much to tie up before I drop off the twig, I wanted to make sure I've got it all out.

I am looking at your photo on my desk as I write this and although you are the epitome of the handsome cheeky chappie with the 'devil may care smile', I cannot help but sense sadness and disappointment in your expression too. As you are now dead and gone, and have been for many years, I can in a way take as much theatrical licence as I like, and write a story to suit my needs as your abandoned daughter.

It sounds very dramatic, doesn't it? It's also not entirely correct, but from what I have learnt you did seem to have made a habit of leaving children lying about! I get the feeling you did not feel empathy with the fruits of your loins. If you were my son I would have told you to be more careful and keep it in your pants! But again I sense you had a need to be loved and wanted by women, and then when the dratted children came along they got in the way and stole the attention away from you. You are not alone in this. I think quite a fair percentage of men feel neglected if the truth be known, and they probably have good reason to be.

However, I want you to understand that I understand, and it is a great regret to me that we could never meet because I think you would have liked me. From all the information we have about you, I cannot tell if you had other daughters; I am sure you must have done even if you didn't know about them, but maybe meeting them might have helped you get back on track.

You were obviously the golden boy as a baby. You were loved to pieces and, dare I say it, spoiled rotten. You must have felt like the world was going to be your oyster. When you went off to Europe in 1916 you were so young; what dreams you must have had then. Yet you came back to the same old, same old. Why did you not escape like Leona did? You might have become a film star – you certainly had the looks. What happened to you, Carl? Was it the war? So many young men seemed to lose their nerve or their zest for life after seeing so much death and destruction. You got married to Helen when she was four months' pregnant – was that what put a stop to your ambition?

It is so strange because I can see in you so much of what I used to go for as a young woman, the bad choices I made with boyfriends. You are a Gemini like me. You were born 1 June, I was born 31 May. I had two Gemini boyfriends who both broke my heart because they could not commit. The first love of my life was called Karel (Czechoslovakian spelling), how is that for a coincidence? The second, in my twenties, was an actor who was always cheating on me. Then I married a man who had a constant stream of women and made me feel so small and insignificant I tried to commit suicide, just like your sister Leona did. Were you there for her then, I wonder? Then I married a man who really seemed to dislike women, and I feel had some thing in common with you in that I always felt he had to be the centre of the universe and would shout and scream if that didn't happen. However, he did give me two beautiful sons and, unlike you, I engaged with them and made them part of my life, and they have kept me alive through thick and thin.

My biggest problem has been to try and teach them how to be strong independent men, with hearts, and not let them think men are weak if they love a woman. I finally found the right man in 2004 and, dear Father, I wish you could have met him just as indeed I wish my adopted father Donald Bellingham could have met him too. He is kind and strong and, though he can be pig-headed and self-opinionated, he has a huge heart of gold and has taken us all on. How I can be so mean as to die on him is beyond my understanding.

Talking about my other father, Donald Bellingham, brings me to the subject of nurture over nature. My dear dad (we will always assume I am referring now to Donald) was my hero. He was of a generation that no longer exists, I fear. He fought in the Second World War, in Bomber Command and was very brave and decorated for his war efforts. But he was also incredibly shy and self-effacing. People sometimes took this to be a weakness but that was always a big mistake. He was uncompromising in his outlook, though I like to think he was fair. I gave both my parents such grief as a teenager and used to say that it was all in my genes. Strangely I blamed my mother's side and suggested because she gave me up for adoption she must have been weak and worthless. She probably drank too much and had lots of men, that was my judgement of her. Looking at things now that was more to do with your side of the fence I think, Father dear. I gather from Marjorie that you liked a tipple!

Thank God for my dear old dad. He never let me down. I would ring up in the middle of the night from some party or other and beg him to come and take me home. Oh how many trips must he have made down the M1 in the middle of the night. He had an enormous capacity for love. In fact he was one of the few men I have seen with babies who is not threatened by them, and Mum always said he was brilliant with us when we were little. So you see I had a perfect example to follow and knew exactly what I should be looking for in a husband. But such gems are difficult to find.

I am truly deeply sad that when my sons came along I was in a marriage that restricted my children from seeing their grandparents. It would have made a huge difference to their take on life, I think, if they could have spent time on the farm with my parents, especially Dad. Only now am I beginning to understand what being a grandparent is all about. It is not, in my opinion, filling your time with your grandchildren because you have no other life, nor is it about babysitting endlessly while your daughter or son goes off to work to earn more money to have a bigger house. It is to offer the other side of the coin, the little things maybe that get forgotten in everyday life, like manners, or seeking advice on parts of life that they can't ask their parents about. To me, it is offering a different view of the world and letting your grandchildren know that there is always someone rooting for you. Being a grandparent also gives you a sense of the continuation of life. One thing I think men don't ever quite understand about women and their love for their children and families is that the more love we are asked to give the more we find. I think some men think there just won't be enough to go round and they will miss out. Is that maybe why you could never really commit, Carl?

But oh, what joy would you have now if you could see your great-grandson smiling into the camera exactly as you did as a little boy. I am trying to make sure that Sacha knows he will always have another family here with us if he needs an option – never taking away from his mother, who has done a fine job of bringing him up. It saddens me that Sacha is from a broken family too, so one thing I can do and I am doing is trying to leave my family a strong legacy that will bind them together. My parents were adamant we should always be loyal to each other. I remember my mother being very pedantic about the wording of her will in which she wanted it stressed that all her estate was to be divided 'amicably' between us three girls. We would take the mickey and tell her that had we wished to fight there would be nothing she could do about it!

So I have nearly finished my little parcel of words which have helped me to tie up loose ends. There is a pain in my heart that I have to leave all my beloved family. Maybe we are meant to have a dialogue, you and I, to get together once this lifetime is over, but I wish you could have been more patient and left me alone a while longer to allow me to make sure all my boys will be OK. But then I suppose they have to carry on the legacy now, don't they. If it is all too neatly tied up there will be nothing left of our family's story for them to take forward.

I hope you can look down and see my world. I have worked so hard to get it right before I go and I hope there is a way you can look after them all, just as I will be doing from wherever I am off to. Who knows we might just meet in the middle.

Lots of love

Lynda B x

22
TIME WILL TELL

....

August 2014

It is another fragrant summer's day and I just cannot believe I am going to die soon. This whole year has been surreal and, in fact, given that the time allotted for most people with this stage of cancer is two years, I have already got halfway, which is great. I really am in a good place, all things considered, but yet, as I write this, I feel like screaming with the frustration of it all, and I think that is because, very slowly in the last couple of weeks, the effects of the chemo are getting to me more than they have before. My mouth is full of ulcers, so apart from the fact I can't taste most food anymore anyway, I now can't eat anything because it is so sore. I'm also suffering from thrush in the throat, which has made my voice go thin and reedy and that upsets me, because one of the things I have been able to do since I've been ill so far is the odd voice-over, so soon I won't be able to do that either. Having said that, I did recently get a call to do a voice-over on the radio for re-writing of wills. My voice-over agent, Helen, was hysterical when she rang, she was all apologetic about it, saying, 'Lynda, this is not a wind-up, I didn't realise until I was ringing you what you might think about doing this, babe. Is it uncomfortable for you?'

I laughed, 'No, of course it's not, it is actually something I know a good deal about now, Helen, and I am delighted someone has asked for me. Thanks, I will be there.'

So you see? Every time I think I am finished and I have been tossed aside, something comes up. I am also editing the celebration edition to mark forty years of *Yours* magazine, which is great fun.

But even though I am finding the chemo is taking its toll, I don't want you all to think I am feeling sorry for myself, I just want to paint an honest picture of how things are progressing. So let us go back to the dreaded chemo effect and the Avastin that makes everything bleed, from my nose to my stoma to my bottom. I know, folks, it is all going on up here in North London. However, when I stop whingeing and get up and at it, I am almost fine.

We had a lovely lunch yesterday with my eldest son and Sacha, and my sister came and my friend Pat too. I had cooked a whole salmon and made chocolate mousse for pud. I actually put some make-up on so my son Michael could have a nice photo of me and Sacha. We made a plan to go to Legoland sometime soon and I went to bed full of hope.

Then I woke at three and the darkness took over and I got so frightened. I don't want to leave my husband Michael, because I know he is going to be so lonely. I know Brad and Stacey will rally round, and I hope my two do as well. But he can be a cantankerous old bugger at times, and I don't want him to put everybody off! Then there is my sister, who has had so much sadness in her life the last ten years, and now I am going to leave her too. Mind you, that could be a relief for her, no more running round finding me plastic jugs and taking me to cake shops. My sweet tooth has really taken over lately, and Jean and I find amazing purveyors of cakes to feed our habit.

The one thing Jean and I do keep putting off is going through my jewellery. Don't get me wrong, there is hardly a hidden treasure trove of diamonds, but I do like things to go to the right people, and there are things in my trinket box that have certain people's names on them, whether they are valuable or not. I also think it is a job, just like going through a loved one's clothes, that can be so distressing for the person left behind, so if I can make things easier for everyone then I will. I am always having clear-outs now – it is a great way of assuaging any guilt one might have about buying something new if you can give away something else to a friend in the meantime.

Mind you, I have to psyche myself up to go into one of those second-hand shops because I sometimes just want to hit the saleswomen in there. The snobbery is unbelievable in some of these establishments. I suppose I live in one of the worst areas, being Hampstead and Highgate, but honestly it makes me so mad. The shops are often full of disgusting designer garb to start with, like the worst indulgences of Roberto Cavalli on speed, and they have the gall to turn their noses up at a brand-new evening dress I bought in John Lewis, a brand new, size twelve, black dress.

'Sorry, Madam, just not for us, I am afraid, and really a size too large,' simpered the woman in a bright yellow dress which clung to her fat bits! I am sorry to be so mean but really people should take a reality check sometimes. Still, it is good to have these things in hand while I am able to do them myself.

Then there are the boys. My beautiful boys who give me grief but also so much joy. I have told them that I do really believe that they will benefit from my death in ways they will not recognise until later in life. I will leave them my energy, which is why I don't want to hang about once everything kicks in and starts to fall apart. I want them to remember me as I was at my best: fighting, laughing, crying and being theatrical maybe, but that is part of me.

Looking at the photos of my real father I realise I was right to feel there had to be an emotional connection somewhere with my birth family, but I had taken the wrong path originally. It was the male side that was calling me, and interestingly my whole life, looking back now, has been surrounded by men! Yes, I was adopted by a family of girls but I then gave birth to boys and joined the land of lads. My birth mother, Marjorie, on the other hand, is the sensible side but also the weak side, in that she did not find herself either but instead lived a lie and let other people tell her what to do. I forgive her but not the rest of that family.

I just want my children to find themselves and take the good with the bad. I am frustrated because I think I still have a great deal to discover about myself, and my family, and I do feel cheated. I really know nothing about my birth family at all apart from some 'interesting' facts. My aunt committing suicide brings back my own terrible loneliness in 1976 when my first marriage broke down. I had no work and a mortgage to pay, and the man I had loved thought I was worthless. The thin thread in my heart is there though now, and I understand Luella and her suicide. I do believe it is a very selfish act though and I would never have done it to my sons.

I feel differently when it comes to my beloved Mum and Dad Bellingham. The thing that really sticks out is that I loved them as people, just as much as I did as parents, and I don't think many people can honestly say that.

And then we come back to my relationship with my boys. Do we ever know our children? Since dealing with my cancer, Robert often comes up and gives me this quiet intense hug, and just looks at me. It is as if he is trying to memorise my face for when I am gone. My elder son, Michael, who is much more extrovert, does it with phone calls, and when he comes to visit he is all bonhomie – but now there is a sadness and a small panic in his eyes, and I know he is thinking about life without me. That is not a bad thing for him to learn because he is that sort of man. I want him to find a woman who will really 'look after him'. He needs that security and she will benefit. If he is happy and secure he will be a wonderful husband. That much I do know.

I am lucky to have found Niki Pittman, my second cousin in Missouri, and I think it is great for the boys to have another family line to follow. They certainly are a mixture: Italian father, half-American and half-Canadian mother, with a strong British influence from my wonderful adopted Mum and Dad, Don and Ruth Bellingham. They really do make the case for nurture over nature any day of the week. It is because of the legacy of my dear family

Bellingham that I shall continue to fight on and try whatever comes along to keep me here as long as possible to see the fruits of my labours, because of them that I have two strong and successful and deep-down lovable sons.

Sadly, we discovered I am not suitable for the test drugs they wanted to put me on, but I went to see a very interesting man called Erdal Mehmet who introduced me to a PMF machine, which has something to do with magnets and breaking up the blood cells in my body. I did try the magnets for a month, and I had hoped that when I went to the clinic again I would see my markers had gone down, but sadly I don't think I am going to be here long enough for them to take hold. I do recommend anyone in the early stage of cancer to go and talk to him.

I am not negative at all and I enjoy every day I wake up. It has been an especially uplifting month because the weather has been so wonderful. I know most people are not sleeping at night because of the heat but one of the upsides for me has been my pins and needles and poor circulation, which has resulted in my feeling cold! How good is that?

13 August 2014

Yesterday was the glorious 12th. The grouse season began dear? Oh you don't do game, what a shame.

What a load of b—! But most appropriate in my case. The glorious 12th will be remembered in our diary because it was the day I decided when I will die.

I am very dramatic, aren't I? I know it is not ultimately my decision but it is my last vestige of control of myself to sit in front of the oncologist and say when I would like to stop having chemo and let the natural way do its thing.

It has been a rather fast deterioration over the last couple of weeks and bizarrely it has been the desire to finish this book that has both spurred me on and finished me off! I am on such strong chemo now that my body is finally protesting. I have ulcers all over the inside of my mouth. I have them in my throat too so my voice is going, which I find especially hard because my voice has been my trademark. I recently went to see a psychic and he was wonderful and told me I would go when I was ready and when I had finished all the jobs I had to do. He was saying I had much longer, but I think he was trying to make that so, bless him. I have been to readings a couple of times and they have always been incredibly enlightening.

Because I was in such pain and discomfort I decided to go into the clinic and get some help with the symptoms. This is something I have not done all year because I wanted to deal with things by myself. But now the cancer – or rather the chemo – was getting to me. That morning as I was waiting for Michael to go to the clinic a catalogue dropped through the letter box. Now here's a test. To order, or not to order? Would it be a waste of money to get a handbag or a pair of boots? It's a problem don't you think? You don't think about all these little moments until they are upon you and your life is on the way out. Well I grappled with the problem for a nanosecond and ordered a handbag and a jacket. Well for goodness sake, chaps, I was hardly wasting the family fortune, and I knew that when the doorbell rang a few days later it would bring me such joy it was worth the guilt.

So I went to get some pills from my regular doctor, Dr di Cesare, who is so kind and helpful. I was telling him about my book and what did he think about my options, and how long did he think I had got left? Sometimes I really cannot believe I am stage four and terminal.

His response was much like everyone else's. I could go on for months. No one knows. That is my problem. No one knows.

Except I do now. I sat down with Michael, Professor Stebbing and Ani and announced: 'The time has come to cease and desist. I would love to make one more Christmas, if possible, but I want to stop taking chemo around November in order to pass away by the end of January.' Of course things may not pan out as I have decided now but it was such a relief to say the words.

Please don't think I am giving up for the sake of a few ulcers, it is the fact that my body has started to rot and I promised myself that as soon as that happened I would make a plan. I want my family to remember me whole. I want you all to remember me!

How embarrassing it would be if I do go on for years. Can you imagine the abuse I would get on Twitter? That Lynda Bellingham conned us into thinking she was dying so we would buy her book! Mind you, the positive side of staying alive – apart from the fact I would be alive – is there could be a third book in the Lynda Bellingham Trilogy entitled:

Hang on! There's something I forgot to mention . . .

Epilogue
LETTERS TO MY LOVED ONES

....

When I wrote my letter to my father for this book, I unlocked something within and I realised it would help me, and my family, to do the same for the rest of the men in my life now. And so I set about writing these letters to my sons, stepson and dear husband Michael.

Letter to the boys

Dear Michael and Robbie,

Michael, there is a photo of you as a baby and I seem to be presenting you to the world and you are responding beautifully, like the actor you are, with a big beaming smile. We both look very sparkly if you can understand my meaning. Then there is a photo of me and you, Robbie, when you were a baby at a very similar age, five years later, and here I am again trying to present my new son, but this time you are having none of it, Rob. You are gazing into the camera slightly miffed and a bit uncertain of what is required of you, and I am looking unsure of my ability to make you feel secure, and I look sad and actually that is exactly how it was in 1988.

I am not going to go back over wasted years but I guess they have to be taken into the equation of where you both are today. I take responsibility for giving you a fractured life. Well, I take some of the responsibility, but I also take the pride and joy I get from your existence and how you have turned out. You are both so different yet from the same mould. I love you both so much it hurts. I think it is hard for men to understand how emotion works in women, because as far as I can make out men are so much more uncomplicated, simple, and I don't mean that in a derogatory way at all. Men need very little to make them happy whereas women need to pick and unpick and put back together again.

I wish I had been tougher with you both about the obvious stuff in life, but I really thought you were both clever enough to see what had to be done. If you didn't do your homework you would fail exams, if you didn't tell the truth we would push each other away, if you do bad things they will come back to haunt you.

Somehow you have both managed to reach a point where this has all become clear to you, and now you can move forward and make great lives for yourselves. The terrible truth is I will not be there to enjoy those moments. I am so sorry, but if you have a little spirituality in you, believe I will be watching.

When my dad and mum died so soon after each other I felt like an orphan but I did have you both to look after. Michael, you have Sacha and he really does need you. I know it is so tough to deal with him and you have no nice added extras like a lovely home or money to take him places, but they will come. Have faith in yourself. Hopefully

I have taught you to aspire to the good things in life and that isn't just about money, it is what is in your soul. Please listen to your brother – he is a wise guy behind that quizzical regard.

Robbie, you have Michael to look after. I know that is not what you want to hear and nor does Michael! But it is the truth, for the time being anyway. Open your heart to Michael, Robbie, he is not like you. He is a bit theatrical and self-obsessed but that is what actors are like! However, he is also part of me and I hope my legacy will teach him to reach out to others, forget himself and listen to what others have to say. I mean really listen, Michael, not keep quiet as you plan your next sentence or tirade while they are speaking. Do I seem harsh? Maybe, but it is only because I love you both so much and if I thought you were not going to help each other through this I would die. Ha ha!

When I was writing this I got a call from you, Michael, and it was so insightful and perceptive of you. You knew something was wrong and you were fearful and had to ring to check up. The interesting thing was that Michael (Hubbie) and I had discussed on the way home from the clinic whether to tell you and Robbie our thoughts following my appointment or leave you in blissful ignorance until Christmas. You solved that problem for me the moment you rang, because that is how we work as a family. Michael Pattemore finds that hard, I think, and keeps things close to his chest. But he has to understand we work differently and I am glad it is all out in the open, because then there is no strain on me to watch what I say or do.

My decision to stop the chemo is personal and probably the only thing I have left to myself. I know you boys will be upset and probably go through a cross period with me, but you have to respect my needs. I know you do.

I know you will both feel very abandoned and I can't help you through that, but one thing I can assure you is that Michael loves you both very much and he will need you as much as anybody because you are his link to me. We are all very different people and will not always see eye to eye – that much we know already – but what I can see from a distance is a group of men who have one thing in common, and it makes you listen to the others, and it makes you realise you are not the only person on the planet and there are other ways of living life. Sometimes the road we choose changes dramatically and we have to adapt pretty sharpish or we get lost. That is what I am trying to give you, I suppose, a view of life – and in this case, death – that you can adapt. You are both so amazing and, believe me, you are very strong.

When the moment comes to say goodbye let's just hold hands and love each other, as we surely do.

Letter to stepson

Hello Stepson,

I always smile when I say that because people must think how strange to call you in such a cold and removed way. But if you remember we had a laugh about it once when I was texting you about coming home for dinner and we laughed that a girlfriend might see the text and think I was another woman! So I became the Evil Stepmother. I have known you a small part of your life but a very important few years. You were nineteen when you arrived off that plane looking like a Beverly Hillbilly! I remember whispering to Michael, 'Oh my God, is that him?'

You have changed so much, Brad, and for the better in every way. You have helped me understand my two. I have been much tougher on you than I ever was with Michael and Robbie. It is easier in a way because I am not your mother, or sister, or whatever. I met you as a person in your own right and had to get to know you. With our own children we just assume a knowledge of them as they are growing up. This is completely wrong, of course, and I realise as I write this that I am writing to a young man I have come to know and love.

It has been difficult for you, I know, to come here and live a completely different life, but you have coped brilliantly. I hope that your mum will understand that in no way does this lessen her place in your life, that will always be sacred, and I hope that through our relationship you have learned more about your mum and maybe even your dad and what they went through.

I also need to say that I cannot include your sister Stacey in much of what we talk about because I don't know her as well. But again, I think you will be able to help her, Brad, in ways that no one expects of you, because you have seen so many different sides of life that you might never have done if you had just stayed in America. Well, that is a definite – you know what I feel about Americans in general, or rather Middle America where the sun don't shine!

Stacey needs to stand on her own two feet, which is bloody tough I know, but you can help her. She will probably hate me for saying this, but Stacey, I have learned so much from being surrounded by all these men. Your boys need more than just their father now. They need granddads and uncles to give them a balanced view of what being male is all about. When I split up from Michael and Robbie's dad, they had no one male to turn to. My father was not well, and anyway they had been put off their grandparents by my ex because I think he felt threatened by them. Brad is your bridge, if you like, to other paths in life and this is what I keep banging on about, because it is so important to learn as much as we can about how life works.

Brad, you have been amazing these past couple of years and you will reap the benefits for the rest of your life. I admire your ambition and desire for the good things in life, just don't forget to feed your soul.

D.H. Lawrence said, 'Money poisons you when you've got it, and starves you when you haven't.'

Get out there and reach for the stars; you can do it but never settle for second best.

Just one more thing . . . Please look after your dad. He will need you very much and don't argue with him, just agree and say, 'Yes, Daddy knows best' and he will be as happy as a Somerset hog in s—!

To Michael

Remember:
That morning in Spain,
The full English going down a storm.
'You want a mortgage?

There's Something I've Been Dying to Tell You

Not a problem Miss B.'
Already an intimacy,
A connection with a like soul.
Watching me in your car mirror, your flash
     hairdresser's car!
Sussing me out, weighing me up.

Remember:
A day of laughter and sunshine,
And way too much wine,
Then goodbye and thanks and back to London for me,
You returned to the bar for another glass of Riscali.
Then texts and phone calls,
An invitation from me,
To dinner, anytime.
'Your daughter is with you?'
Oh damn . . . How lovely!
'Bring her as well,
Not a problem at all.'

Remember:
Instant contact, electricity and passion,
Certainly lust and possibly need?
Reaching out for affection, while grappling to find
That still small voice that says
What?
Ah now we have it
A sentence so simple
So hard to define
To learn to trust once again
To step over that line.

Lynda Bellingham

Remember:
Then came death to our beginnings
Losing my parents in one month
I quickly found you
The centre, the nub of it all
My rock, my knight, my lover.
You made me wake up and grab the life
That was offered, so real and so different
From the sham I was living.
So alone and so lonely
Just me and my boys.
Thank God for my boys.
Could you breach that wall of motherly love?
Not easily, but you did.

Remember:
Truth and lies?
People trying to crush us with their cynical mediocrity
Their sad distorted negativity.
'Not a problem,' you'd say
'Not a problem at all.'
You can do anything
Heal a wound or burst a boil
Life does not scare you
Not nothing at all.
But death does, doesn't it, my lover?
Death is unfair and cruel
Not in your remit at all.

Remember:
How we talked of our life together

There's Something I've Been Dying to Tell You

When all our chores had been done
Twenty years, fifteen at least
To open our box of ten years together
Yes short but oh so sweet.
Don't give up now, my lover.
Do some of the things we promised we would do
Please guard the door and the lid to our trinkets
Our box of 'remembers'.

Remember:
You always aim for the best
We have had it and you will keep alive, though I'm
    dead.
It's only a word so say it, spit it out
Toss it away in the wind
Think only of good things and now this is it
I have come to the point, round and round I go
They are almost unspeakable
So precious have they grown
As always I tell you
In my own way
I love you Michael Pattemore
There's nothing more I can say.